Yale University – New Haven, Connecticut

If I have seen further than others, it is by standing upon the shoulders of giants.

Sir Isaac Newton

THE AUTHENTIC

SHOWING COLLEGES YOU'RE
MORE THAN A NUMBER

Our goal is to help you distinguish yourself beyond your GPA and test scores by helping you discover how to find the connections that can lead you to a successful college experience, a meaningful career, and a joyful life.

KATRIN MUIR LAU | JUDITH WIDENER MUIR

PREVIOUS BOOKS BY THESE AUTHORS

FINDING YOUR U: Navigating The College Application Process
Katrin Muir Lau & Judith Widener Muir

LIVE WIRES: Neuro-Parenting to Ignite Your Teen's Brain
Judith Widener Muir

Copyright @2023
All rights reserved.
ISBN: 979-8-9887243-0-8
Library of Congress Number: Pending
www.educationalplan.com

Roni Atnipp, Editor
Elise DeSilva, Design, Limb Design
Rob Muir, Photographer
Printed in the United States of America by Bayside Printing Company, Inc.

In the making of this book, every attempt has been made to verify names and facts. We apologize if any errors have been made.

CONTENTS

Rice University – Houston, Texas

The pessimist complains about the wind.
The optimist expects it to change.
The leader adjusts the sails.

John Maxwell

A MESSAGE ABOUT OUR PURPOSE

Science now confirms that students learn best with an adult who makes lessons relevant and interactive. A strategically planned and personally appropriate experience with a mentor in an area where you have a personal interest and an aptitude can help you learn about the world you will enter — and, even more importantly, learn about yourself.

For multiple decades, worried parents and anxious teens have come to us as college counselors to help them choose the best fit in a college and a future career. We assist in seeing what others might miss, finding creative ideas that can tap into their aptitudes and interests because the college application process has become more complex, less transparent, and highly nuanced. We help families get past the media hype that can startle, unsettle, and confuse.

We listen first. Then we nudge. We want you to ask the best questions and find the most relevant answers as you seek to secure your future — and to be as competitive as possible in the process. We send our students out to discover the world and have a peek at what awaits them.

We have sent thousands of students out into the workforce as interns, mostly unpaid, to chart their future — as private investigators, financial analysts, news correspondents, journalists, photographers, architects — even one student alternating snowshoes and cross country skis while tracking mountain lions in rural Idaho to monitor their predatory habits.

When a student returns from an internship, we smile when we hear professional vernacular creep into their daily conversation. Teenagers using terms or ideas like thoraco-abdominal aortic aneurysm, splenectomy, androgynous peripheral docking system, price-earnings ratio, graphical user interface means that an internship or working with a mentor is rubbing off.

Whether through donning green surgical scrubs in a medical center, white lab coats in cancer research labs, wrinkled cotton trader jackets on the floor of the New York Stock Exchange, appendaging clipboards at psychiatric wards, headsets at NASA, or prowling the back rooms of the Metropolitan Museum, students preview what life after college might entail when they hit the job market running. We watch career interests blossom as students step out of their classrooms and into newsrooms, operating rooms or boardrooms across the city, the nation, the world.

Students witness the nuance of business negotiation, the intensity of criminal prosecution, the volatility of the stock market, the competitive edge of new technology, the impact of public relations, or the significance of teamwork. They have been surprised at predawn surgery schedules, the requisite portion of busy work each profession entails, and the remarkable long hours focused managers sustain. They experience how important first impressions are, how crucial critical details can be, and how imperative preparation will lead to a satisfying and productive professional future.

We write now as college admission experts sharing what you need to know. We will share what we have learned over our past years of working together — as a mother and daughter team, ushering our own family members through their college years, as well — to save you time and give you hope.

Katrin & Judy

University of Oxford – Oxford, England

BECOMING THE AUTHENTIC U

We graduated from college decades ago, but we now spend most of our waking hours thinking about the current college admission process: what leads to successful applications, but more importantly, what leads to a successful fit between student and school. In our previous book, *Finding Your U: Navigating the College Admission Process*, we shared what we have learned about the importance of applying to the colleges and universities that will prepare you for the life you want to live, rather than choosing a school with a high number on a ranking list. We have come to realize that in the admissions process, the end goal is not just to go to college but also to prepare for a meaningful life. As our clients have gone on to attend the colleges of their choice, we realized that even in the admission process, the end goal is not to go to college, but to prepare for a successful life.

We realized that our advice turned out to be much bigger than just about college when we advised students to take the time to focus on who they really are and to look for people working in the fields that interest them. It's an age-old concept — you apprentice yourself to a master craftsman in a specific field of personal interest, and through exposure and practice, you gain skills and experience that lead you to opportunity. And these relationships don't just help you to get a peek into a career through an internship — when handled well, they lead to lasting connections that can help you understand yourself better, increase your chances of being accepted at the college of your choice, and prepare you for the most joyful life possible. The students who took this advice to heart are thriving, years beyond college graduation.

The Past Becomes The Present

While we were gathering our notes for this book, we discovered the letters from John H. Muir, our father-in-law/grandfather. As a high school student in 1923, he realized that he was interested in becoming a naval architect. So what did he do? He sat down and typed up a letter to someone he felt might be the best source, asking for specific advice about the best path to this career. As we read the letters, we realized how quickly these distinguished men were ready to help a young person seeking knowledge.

Yes, the world has changed dramatically since 1923, but in our extensive experience working with more than 5,000 students over the past thirty years, we see clearly that successful people want to help the next generation, especially the young people emerging who share their particular interests. The best preparation you can make to get into college is not to agonize over your test scores and take and retake your SAT hoping for a few points jump. The best preparation you can make is to spend time actively thinking about who you are, connecting the dots between your interests and the careers that exist in those areas, and seeking relationships with people who are in those careers. These experiences will provide you with tools that will help you achieve admission, maximize your time at college, and ensure that you set off on a career path that will bring you fulfillment. And isn't that what it's all about?

December 13, 1923.

Frank E. Kirby, N. A.
Tuller Hotel,
Detroit, Mich.

Dear Sir:

I am a boy, fifteen, in the second year of high
school and I have decided that I want to be a Naval Architect.
In order to more fully prepare myself to be a Naval Architect,
I am sending you the following questions whose answers will
help me to decide on my future course in high school and college.

What do you think of Naval Architecture as a profession for a young man to enter?

What college would you recommend for Naval Architecture?

Should a course in Naval Architecture be taken as a
post-graduate course or directly upon leaving high school?

What is the best Foreign language to take in high
school in preparation for Naval Architecture?

I have taken Latin for two years (half the course).
Should I continue it or drop it for some other language?

Which is more important to a Naval Architect, che-
mistry or physics?

What is the procedure upon leaving college to become a Naval Architect?

My high school principal, Mr. Edwin L. Miller, and
my dad who was paymaster and timekeeper at the Detroit Shipbuilding Company have suggested that I write to you, and you
will spare the time to answer these questions. I will be very
grateful.

Yours truly,

John H. Muir, Jr.
602 Blaine Ave.,
Detroit, Mich.

As a high school student in 1923, John H. Muir aspired to become a naval
architect. So, he sat down and typed a letter to someone he felt could
give him worthy advice for the best path to this career — and amazingly, the
Secretary of the Navy responded!

JOHN H. MUIR became the naval architect/marine engineer who designed the first electronically controlled valve system, first implemented on the storage tanks on the Esso Huntington. The tanker carried liquids; valves controlled the flow through the hoses for loading and unloading cargo. Muir's innovation meant that crew members did not have to manually open and close the valves on the deck, but controlled them from an enclosed area below the ship's bridge, providing more efficiency and speed, especially in inclement weather and at night.

He came up with an elaborate color scheme on the panel that so enamored the crew that they chose to paint all the pipes and valves on the deck to match the control board.

During WWII, Muir was not allowed to join the Navy; instead, he was directed to work for the Maritime Commission in Washington, DC, using his skills to design and improve propellers to get more speed out of the ships with the hope of avoiding being torpedoed by submarines.

THE SECRETARY OF THE NAVY.
WASHINGTON.

December 22, 1923.

My dear Ed:

I have your letter of December 13th in reference to a young man by the name of John Muir. I made inquiry of the Chief Constructor of the Navy, and he stated that young Muir would not need Latin in order to become a Naval Architect. However, a knowledge of Latin would be helpful in acquiring other foreign languages, such as French and Italian, which are useful to one following the profession of a Naval Achitect as many technical books are in those languages.

With the season's best wishes, I am

Sincerely yours,

Edwin Denby

Mr. Edwin L. Miller,
    Supervising Principal,
        Detroit High Schools,
            Detroit, Michigan.

ABSOLUTELY FIREPROOF

COR. PARK, ADAMS AND BAGLEY AVES.

ADDRESS ALL BUSINESS COMMUNICATIONS TO HOTEL TULLER

HOTEL TULLER
European Plan

TULLER HOTEL CO.
O.C. FROMAN
MANAGER

DETROIT, MICH.

January 7, 1924

Mr. John H. Muir, Jr.,
602 Blaine Avenue,
Detroit, Mich.

My dear Master Muir:-

Replying to yours of the 31st ult., which came during my absence in New York:

1st: There will always be work in this country for naval architects and marine engineers.

2nd: No better college than the University of Michigan.

3rd: My feeling is that naval architecture should be a post-graduate course, though of course it might be taken immediately after high school.

4th: French best for theory and German best for practical shipbuilding.

5th: French or German instead of continuing with Latin.

6th: Physics:

7th: Start work in a shipyard mould loft and continue with a platers' gang until you have worked off your thumbs.

With best wishes for your success, I am,

Very truly yours,

Frank E. Kirby

Though John H. Muir lived and worked a century ago, his approach to making connections with his interests and the individuals who were living the life he envisioned is still the most fundamentally sound path to success. What does his approach look like in today's world?

We must step up and reach out to propel our lives forward. Through guiding thousands of students over many years, we have found that this approach still prevails.

In the following pages we will share with you what we teach our students: how you make the leap from high school to college and then to the life you envision for yourself.

We will show you how to discover and promote the authentic **YOU** to the world.

THE SUCCESS SEQUENCE

From the postwar era to today, the idea has been cemented that teenagers graduate from high school, earn a college degree, secure a job, and move out of their childhood home. They launch into adulthood when they finish school, start a job, get married, buy a home, then begin a family — a concept deemed "the success sequence."

Today, many teenagers still go to college; but then, regardless of whether they choose a job-related major, they drift through jobs after graduation — short of money, minus any real plan — and often land back in their parents' proverbial basement. This lengthy take-off is relatively new. Today's parents share their anxiety about their children's stumble toward independence.

The "success-sequence" trend of a quick launch into adulthood is ending, and definitions of success are changing. Census figures show that the number of 19-24 year olds living with their parents is edging up — in 1960 it was 30%, in 1980 it was 35%, and as we write, it is 47%. What has caused these delays in reaching the milestones of adulthood, and what can you do to position yourself for stability, growth, and authentic success in the face of these winds of change?

Today you are asked to declare a major and demonstrate a fit for a college program to garner the nod from admission deans at many highly selective colleges. You are asked to plan for a career in order to choose the right college to have the right major to get the right job — all before you turn seventeen. Colleges lament that their enrollment is based on the whims of seventeen-year-olds.

So how can you prepare to know yourself and to know the job market that lies somewhere beyond your front door?

Don't despair. While we strongly believe that you are your own best advocate and need to do the work yourself, we also believe that learning from others and their experience is one of the best ways to reach your goals. We have had front row seats to more admissions stories than we can begin to count, and we have learned what really works. And it really works because it is what matters most. Contrary to how it might feel right now, you are not alone in this discernment process, nor are you competing against everyone else. What we outline here will help you understand yourself and your goals better — and this perspective will provide you with focus, maximize the use of your time, and give you hope as you apply to college and prepare for a career.

Admission Policies Are Changing

Colleges are scrutinizing their current admission policies, reading applicants in the context of their school, family circumstances, and community challenges more than ever.

Test-optional policies are under fire. The expanding role of artificial intelligence will likely compel colleges to expand their format in reviewing applicants beyond the traditional numbers and college essays to assess academic subject mastery, potential to graduate, aptitudes and interests, and what an applicant might contribute to their college community, both as a student and a future alum.

Platforms are shifting. Colleges are looking for new ways for students to share their voices and to articulate their aspirations. For you to identify and enroll in a college that will be a good fit for you and for your future, understanding these disruptions is imperative.

University of Cambridge – Cambridge, England

WHAT SCHOOLS DON'T TEACH

Regardless of their academic journey, too many college graduates miss the on-ramp to careers as they approach graduation. They fail to build a business plan for their lives and don't seek the experiences that lead to their aspirations. They have neglected to build the professional network from whence cometh the job offers.

High schools are not always teaching you what you need to know to tackle college admissions, and colleges aren't always preparing you for the job market. They might teach what materials you should present — your introductory email, your cover letter, your resume — but they aren't teaching interpersonal skills and how to manage the effective interactions with admissions officers and potential employers. These are the details that make it easier for the gatekeepers to know who you are quickly — and help them gauge how much you want to be there, with them, at their place.

In Pursuit Of An Education

Why are your parents and significant adults so worked up about college?

Parents feel that education is the one gift they can give you, one that you will not lose and that no one can take away. Educational credentials can keep you steady during unprecedented economic storms and provide the foundation of skills and trust that can assure you of a fresh start, regardless of any global or personal upheaval you may encounter along the way.

For some of you, your parents started thinking about schools even as they tucked in the first sheet on the mattress of your crib, anticipating your arrival. They thought they could secure the future for their progeny by planning for their education.

Then why is it often difficult for parents and kids to talk about college?

Full of love and replete with noble goals, your parents entered the fray. All too soon it hit: College Admission — words that conjure excitement and hope, but also infuse confusion, concern, complexity — along with overwhelming cost. Just as you do, they face a labyrinth of confusing perspectives.

Since your parents were your age, the college admission process has become more complicated, less transparent, and highly nuanced — and even more so recently as a result of a global pandemic, economic chaos, and rampant racial tension.

We want more graduates to leave college ready to succeed in the competitive global marketplace.

Your parents continue to seek the place where you will hopefully

- Come of age in a community of like-minded and aspiring scholars

- Gather to share the deepest thoughts of mankind from across the ages in preparation for adulthood

- Build a network of supportive colleagues with whom you can share trusted exchanges over time

- Find lifelong friends who will diminish grief and double joy as you move along your journey through life together

Learn to tell your story with relevant details. Be authentic.

So, how do you communicate about this? What in your parents' experience is still valid, and what new information do you need to incorporate in your search for these very worthy educational goals? What questions should you both be asking? How do you craft a modern education that will prepare you to meet the world that awaits you? Who will be your teachers, professors, and mentors? What messages will they deliver?

And then, we ask: who is responsible for what your education should look like?

The answer, of course, is you!

University of St Andrews – St Andrews, Scotland

MENTORS
MATTER

LEARNING FROM EXPERTS

During these moments of disruptive change, there is more you need to do beyond the obvious, as you seek to secure your future and find your place in the world that awaits you. We have seen students who have checked every box — SAT courses, good grades, AP classes, extracurriculars — yet not distinguished themselves when it came time to apply to college. Reaching out to connect can be pivotal. Self-directed learning, a phrase we cannot state often enough, means taking it upon yourself to investigate topics you care deeply about in preparation for your future.

Though your parents and your high school teachers have your best interests in mind, and at heart, the life you are preparing to live is yours. And it is imperative that you spend some time thinking about who you are, who you want to become, and how you want to live. Yes, those ideas will morph and develop as you do, but wherever you are in your personal development, there is an authenticity inside you that needs to be respected.

Your adults have knowledge and experience that are very valuable and that can help you to reach your goals. But if you have not considered what your goals are, you may end up pursuing someone else's definition of success, rather than your own, living a life that doesn't quite fit right.

We have guided hundreds of teens through an outreach for self-directed learning. The importance of this practice became apparent to us, even before we got into the profession, as we reflected about how Rob — the husband and father in our family — had experienced the impact of reaching out. His efforts to connect with someone who shared his interests were life-changing for Rob — indeed, for our whole family, and, ultimately, for many others trying to find their own way.

This story, so personal to our family, illustrates the importance that adult mentors can make in our lives.

Judy's Perspective: Rob's Story

Rob converted his bedroom closet into a dry darkroom during high school, when his penchant for creating compelling black and white images began to emerge. There were no classes in his academically rigorous, private school that provided a focus on the arts to nurture this nascent photographer. So, he taught himself by trial and error and sleuthing out the scant instructional manuals he could muster, reading labels on film cartons, and getting the men at the camera store to answer his questions — even when his allowance did not enable him to buy anything from them. His naval architect-marine engineer father encouraged Rob to go to law school — a career predictive of a steady paycheck and comfortable life.

In college, Rob had a double major in English and History — he loved reliving the classic stories. Halfway through college, he discovered the Art Department and convinced a professor who was an amateur photographer with an artistic vision to teach a class — he said if Rob could muster three students, the class could happen. Rob grabbed his roommates. They also pulled in another professor who had previously worked for *National Geographic*. Rob never told his parents he was taking a photography class.

Then Rob encountered the Ansel Adams Exhibit that the college just happened to have during Rob's quiet immersion into photography. He marveled at the power in Adams' black and white images: the way they could relate a story and leave an impression connected with Rob, the inveterate story-teller himself. The Ansel Adams Exhibit changed the trajectory of Rob's life. He graduated with an undeclared third major in Art. Law school never happened.

Five years later, working at a major commercial photography studio in Houston, Rob lacked the fulfillment that he knew photography should be providing. As his wife, I felt his frustration. I also knew his interest was deep; his talent was real; and the studio was not catapulting him forward. One afternoon, in desperation myself, I instinctively — without really thinking about what I was saying — told him to pick up the phone and call Ansel Adams. I began my rant.

"Tell him how his exhibit changed your life. Tell him how desperately you want to learn from him. Tell him how intently you have studied his images, how you have changed the lens through which you view your world as a result of connecting with his images, how you admire the archival quality he has crafted. Tell him how you feel, what you want to learn, how you admire his mastery of his materials. Do something. Take charge of your own learning. Don't wait for the world to come to you. Go out and create your own opportunities."

Maybe I was just tired. We had toddler Chad and new baby Katrin, and I could not handle seeing Rob report for duty daily, falling into a lackluster routine, picking up extra weekend hours doing maintenance tasks at the studio to support our growing family. He needed to use his talent in a meaningful way to achieve the personal fulfillment that he deserved. I suspected Ansel Adams could be the catalyst Rob needed.

Ansel said, YES, come out to Yosemite and spend some time with him. We were both stunned. Rob asked for a leave of absence. We packed up our babies and headed west. After a short time and critiquing Rob's portfolio from college and comparing it to his current work at the studio, Ansel told Rob to quit his job. At first alarmed that Ansel's message dissed his photography, Rob hardly knew what to say. Ansel said Rob had a remarkable eye for lighting and composition, that he would compromise that innate talent if he remained too long at the studio, simply chronicling record shots, not targeting photographs that told a story or delivered a message.

"Go out on your own. Grow your talent. Grow your business. Help your clients deliver their own stories, using your photography as their vehicle to build their brand and draw customers to their doorsteps." Ansel had his own rant for Rob.

Sitting beside Ansel's grand piano outside of his darkroom in his home at Carmel, staring at our baby Katrin on Ansel's lap and toddler Chad playing on the floor with an assortment of darkroom canisters, I was in shock. We had two babies, a leaking roof, a new mortgage — and now Rob was supposed to leave his "job" and go out on his own? What had I done to our family by suggesting Rob call Ansel Adams?!

What I was witnessing was the power of a mentor to impact a career. My first experience with an internship was with my husband. I saw how learning flourishes when someone is engaged in a personally relevant topic with someone who cares.

Over the next three decades, Rob became a leading magazine, advertising and architectural photographer, widely published and highly sought after by clients to build their brand and enrich their sales. Rob continues to create images that communicate, win awards, and get published. Mentored and inspired by the great photographer Ansel Adams, Rob took Adams' advice along with his training and went out to craft images that speak to an audience.

This epiphany about the power of a mentor changed our family's life, and — then — the lives of thousands of teens trying to find their way and secure their future.

> "Involve me, and I learn..."
> Benjamin Franklin

Katrin's Perspective

Growing up with a mom who connected over a hundred seniors to internships every year in her position as Director of Career Development at The Kinkaid School in Houston, you can only imagine how many internships my brother and sister and I have done, too!

My Internships
Congressman, advertising agency, several interior designers, a college admissions office, an art gallery, a judge, a cancer research lab, Sotheby's Auction House, and The National Gallery of Art's Education Department.

My Sister's Internships
Congressman, Senator, an advertising agency, several interior designers, an art gallery, a jeweler, a judge, *The Washington Post*, *National Geographic*, a cancer research lab, a painter, and a private investigator.

My Brother's Internships
Congressman, CBS News with Dan Rather, the sports department at the local CBS affiliate station, investment firm trading desk next to the New York Stock Exchange, Lieutenant Governor of Texas Campaign, Federal Judge, an asset management firm, Houston Economic Development Council within the Houston Chamber of Commerce, World Economic Summit, a publicly-traded waste management company, and the office of the Vice President of the United States.

The three of us overlapped with several internships — sometimes doing them together, but usually doing the same internship in different years. The classic story of us, doing all of these internships, is when I was interning for an advertising agency one summer during college. I had to miss a few days to get my wisdom teeth out. My sister, who was in high school, stepped in and took my place for a few days. First of all, my sister and I look a lot alike — then, unbeknownst to me, she decided to wear the same red with white polka dot outfit that I had worn the day before! We still laugh about how everyone was looking at her funny until someone finally told her that they thought I had worn the same outfit two days in a row — because they didn't know they weren't looking at me! And, this was a very bold-looking outfit!

I enjoyed my time learning new facets about the job world with each opportunity. I think it was invaluable to discover the parts I liked, as well as the parts I didn't like. Everything I learned — from different types of office environments to the skills needed to be successful within a specific career, helped lead me to knowing that for me, I wanted less time behind a desk, the ability to use my creativity, and have new challenges to conquer every day. Interestingly, being in real estate for twenty years, and now being a college counselor working with the unique stories of each student — both my careers have fit those parameters.

So, let's explore how you can find the mentors that you will need in order to discover your own path to a meaningful life.

WHAT WE HAVE LEARNED

We assume that if teachers teach, children will learn. It is time to hang a question mark on assumptions we have held for many years about education. It is time to take charge of learning at a very personal level. People seldom succeed alone. Reaching out for the connections that can expand productivity, increase efficiency, and propel innovation means building relationships with the mentors who are willing to offer counsel, perspective, and share what they have learned to save time, escalate potential, and amplify the processes that work. Trial and error can be a useful learning process and also delay the sweeping changes that every industry yearns to achieve — whether for profit, quality of life, or better products.

The information explosion and digital technology have changed education forever. Teachers now have an array of platforms that offer multiple ways to present new information and assess content mastery to meet learners.

Experience suggests, and science confirms, that kids learn best when they are engaged in personally relevant projects with mentors they perceive care about them — the hallmark of a thoughtfully planned opportunity that can lead to a positive relationship with a well-matched mentor.

America has shifted from an Industrial Economy to a Knowledge Economy to, most recently, a Tech Economy. The educational system has not shifted with the changes. Currently, education is not necessarily training you for the world you will enter, nor preparing you to use discernment in how you select a college, a college major, and a career. Variability in our classrooms is the norm. We must respect the multiple forms of intelligence that enrich and distinguish our educational communities — athletes, artists, nascent scholars with jagged profiles.

Given the digital landscape in which we now live, we have multiple platforms with which to reach each other where we are and deliver a message that can guide us to a path that can lead to a personally fulfilling career.

Self-Directed Learning

Taking it upon yourself to investigate topics you care deeply about, which escalated during the pandemic, is a lifetime venture. Online opportunities abound: webinars, YouTube, TED Talks, edX, Coursera — each adds substance and expands perspective. You are responsible for yourself. You enrich your education with relationships that flourish through emotional connection, whether through platforms such as Zoom or personal outreach.

Pick Up Where Schools Are Stopping

The clarion call is loud and clear. Pick up where schools are stopping, be thoughtful and creative, assemble your thinking partners — and charge ahead to make sense of what awaits you. Develop a strategic plan to create the experiences that will help you flourish, that will help you maximize educational courses by supplementing with internships with caring mentors where learning can be applied and tested out for future relevance.

The Apprenticeship Model

We use this model as we counsel prospective high schoolers seeking their best college fit. We are simply pulling out the old apprenticeship model and renaming and redesigning it to fit our current times, adding it to our plan to personalize education, get the teens we work with job-ready, and help them launch sooner — with more gusto, productivity, and fulfillment.

Relationships Are Pivotal

In the process and over time, we have learned a lot about people, and especially about relationships: how they are pivotal; how they can become a catalyst for a meaningful and productive future; how they offer guidance, support, validation, and the wisdom of life experience. These are the qualities that vulnerable and volatile teens need to sustain the self-reflection that can produce the narratives they must evolve as they seek to secure their future by garnering a nod from a college admission officer, a potential mentor, or a targeted employer.

Be A Lifelong Learner

As college advisors, we know the importance of procuring degrees and certifications. BE A LIFELONG LEARNER is our mantra. We have led many applicants to the right degree, then graduate degree — often, even, through the next several stages of their development. Even some of the parents have asked for a separate session to contemplate their own self-reflection as they chart their future paths as they become empty-nesters. Even more important than the degree that might manifest deeper and stronger credentials — the proverbial harbingers of future success — have been the relationships forged along the way.

How Would You Define Success

When we ask our students for their definition of future success, they respond with words wrapped around feeling important, garnering respect, being in control, having a voice that is heard, sensing appreciation from others because their work could make a difference, identifying opportunities for promotions, seeking financial stability, making money, procuring meaningful relationships, building a close family unit, becoming a caring parent. Noble goals. Goals seldom achieved merely through credentials from the top graduate programs. Goals achieved often through the connections they were developing, frequently with mentors.

Effective Mentors

We define mentors as those who genuinely care about bringing out the best in others — nurturing their development — by sharing their past experiences and the wisdom of their life experiences. Generally, potential mentors share how someone special had believed in them before they believed in themselves. They welcome the opportunity to share advice and guidance. Seldom do people succeed on their own. Effective mentors are committed to helping others become the best version of themselves they can muster.

For a mentoring relationship to be meaningful and productive, the mentee must truly value what their potential mentor has to offer — and manifest that appreciation for them, letting them know that their presence would make all the difference in igniting the mentee's future. Mentees need to respect their mentor's commitment to their profession, their success in their workplace, their leadership, their wisdom. And the fit must be right. If mismatched, the prognosis can be grim. Doing a "list match" with superficial data seldom works. There is so much more to a productive match. The mentor must feel important and appreciated. Interns must also feel in control of their destiny, so a prospective connection needs to be discussed and decided upon together, with a shared vision of what success might look like and how it might be assessed at the end of the experience. Successful relationships require buy-in from both sides. Mentees must be appreciative, committed — and let their mentors see that they feel that way.

Mentoring Relationships Focus On Advice And Nuance

Mentoring is different from teaching or coaching. It is beyond teaching a new skill set or coaching to transcend obstacles. Mentoring focuses on advice and nuance — looking for a better way to do something, seeking meaningful change in outcome, making a more strategic decision. Mentors help prepare people to enter the world that awaits them or realign their personal direction by assessing changes that need to happen, figuring out how to unleash a mentee's contributions, or overcoming problems left to them from earlier generations. These hopefuls have a lot of work ahead of them. Mentors can help a mentee build a network of support that can help catapult their fresh perspective as they tackle the unfinished business ahead.

Mentoring Should Happen Throughout Our Lives

We watch our teens go back intermittently to the mentors with whom they built lifetime relationships, often starting with a high school internship. This pattern carries into their career ladder, as well. They learn to define clearly what their goal is when seeking a mentorship and then assess how they will define the success of the engagement. Sometimes, there is a timely goal, one which seeks new strategies or additional skills. Sometimes the goal is more amorphous, building on personal perspective about staying the course or shifting directions. But, for the sake of both sides, goals should drive the direction and define a projected outcome. Structuring the mentoring experience is helpful to achieve personal goals and time efficiency for both sides. Be clear about expectations, time commitments, deliverables.

People want to make a difference. Good mentors are busy; they don't have time to stop what they are doing and guide nascent scholars seeking to secure their futures. Yet, these insightful mentors know that they can nurture the creative thinkers and change-agents that our world needs if they pause to share the wisdom of their own personal and professional experiences. They want to make a difference — and mentoring is a way to do it. They want to help develop future leaders. In turn, they will likely be reinvigorated because they feel appreciated and heard and important, at a very personal level —

something not always reinforced as they navigate the daily grind of their own profession. It feels good to have someone look up to them for their wisdom and advice. They can assume that their legacy is assured.

In the end, people like to share their journey and the stories of those who have influenced them. Beyond the graduate programs, MBAs, law degrees, and management training certificates are the more subtle lessons that mentoring offers. Hearing what others have overcome, learning what they did that did not work, learning from their mistakes, as well as their victories — adding this human element to the textbook and professional training sessions can accelerate personal success and productivity over time.

> Finding a mentor is the secret sauce that can help you become the best version of yourself.

Internship In Television

I went from working at the assignment desk to working with reporters on breaking stories. Police radios, phones ringing off the hook, cell phones buzzing, texts popping added noise to an already crazy place. Reporters showed me how to find important parts of an interview, how to write a package, and how to edit to prepare a package for the news. I learned how stories to be covered are chosen and how producers fit together a newscast. I met people who were willing to teach me as much as I was willing to learn. No longer is working on the news an abstract idea. I want to pursue a career in this field. My future looks exciting!

Harvard University, Widener Library – Cambridge, Massachusetts

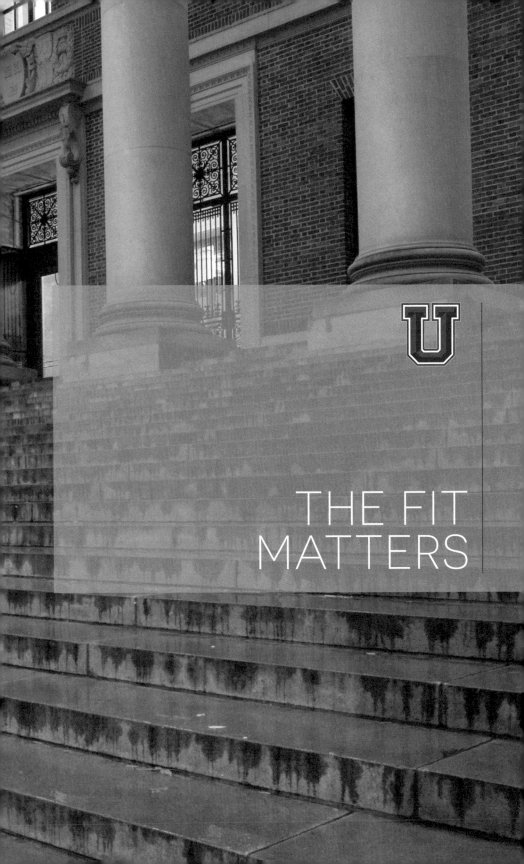

THE FIT
MATTERS

POSITIVE PSYCHOLOGY

The underlying assumption is that fit — what is relevant and appropriate for you — should predict success, which should result in happiness.

Success. Happiness. Two powerful words. Amorphous words. Elusive goals. Concepts that we all chase. All the time.

Fit in a college. Fit in a major. Fit in a mentor. Fit in a career. Why does fit have such potential to keep us steady and productive — then make us happy?

The most popular course in the history of Harvard is Psyc 1504, Positive Psychology. Tal Ben-Shahar taught over 1,400 Harvard students in the spring of 2006 and had 40 Teaching Fellows to manage the numbers. Harvard students were clearly trying to figure out how to achieve happiness. They sought out Ben-Shahar for clues. He espoused that

"…Attaining lasting happiness requires that we enjoy the journey on our way toward a destination we deem valuable." Valuable? Relevant. Meaningful. Fit — there it is again.

Harvard admits students who have garnered profuse accolades; they are the smartest, the fastest, the most accomplished, the most plugged in to hyper-competition. But are they all the happiest? Harvard studies revealed that the personal accolades did not assure happiness or success at Harvard. The greatest predictor of success for students revolved around their social connection — their "fit" with the community. Whether (or not) they felt interconnected and socially supported was directly correlated to outcome at Harvard.

Yale, also concerned for overworked, overstressed students, created an online and in-person course on happiness, as well. Over three million people took Yale's course where they learned the importance of sleep, gratitude, and helping other people. The Yale Happiness Class — Psyc 157, Psychology and the Good Life — is one of the most popular classes offered in Yale's 320-year history. The class had 1,200 students sign up to attend the in-person lecture in the spring of 2018. Moving online, by now over 3.3 million people have signed up, according to the website.

Success And Happiness Relate To How Well We Connect

While individual achievement can garner accolades, our success and happiness can depend on how well we connect with, relate to, and learn from each other. Feeling lonely can be a setback to success. In these complicated, disruptive times in which we live, we will discover that our lone light flashing in the night can be brighter if we shine our lights together.

We are each different. We must find our purpose through self-reflection. The status view of success is not working and is fading. Research is confirming that people really want meaning, purpose, fulfillment. The need to find the fit is real in our society. Meaningful relationships are what people deem most important and where many feel they are failing the most.

Fit matters. Engagement flourishes when the match is right. Success at college is less about personal attributes and more about fitting in. The same rubric often applies to a career environment, as well. Fitting in, making supportive connections, is the best predictor of success.

> "It is not survival of the fittest, rather survival of the best fit."
>
> *Big Potential* by Shawn Achor

Poets write about happiness. Social scientists set up research projects trying to unpack happiness. Developmental psychologists craft inventories to determine who is happy — all trying to figure out how to achieve this state of contentment. Even the famous environmentalist, John Muir, pointed out that everything happens in context.

> "When we try to pick out anything by itself, we find it hitched to everything else in the Universe."
>
> John Muir, The Naturalist

What have we learned from the poets, the scientists, the psychologists, the environmentalists? The recurring message comes back to connection — how everything fits together, in harmony. We are inherently social entities seeking connection, seeking fit.

Relationships can keep us whole, providing a path back to stillness in the times we most need it. We advise our students to choose their friends with hours to live, not hours to kill.

Why do we learn best when we are engaged in a personally relevant project working with someone who cares? Because the connection is there; it results from the fit. Everything happens in context.

The Recurring Message: Fit Matters

We look for the right academic and social fit in a college, the right match in a prospective mentor, the right working environment in a career. Internships with well-matched mentors can be a valuable source for investigation.

The best way to move with gusto into independence — to launch, rather than to drift — is to have a plan, a purpose that has been based on experience, rather than hype. Mentors can be the link, providing the context for self-reflection that can result in self-fulfillment. Internships can then lead you to unpack your unique talents and then follow them to become the best you can be at what you care about the most.

We launch our students with the message that mentors can lead to the fit that builds the connection, which is all powerful. Fit can provide the momentum that keeps positive mindset and hope alive.

> "College is not a costume party; you're not supposed to come dressed as someone else. College is an intense, four-year opportunity to become more yourself than you've ever been. What you need to show us is that you're ready to try."
>
> Massachusetts Institute of Technology (MIT) Admissions Blog

THE
APPRENTICE'S
SECRET

BUILDING MEANINGFUL RELATIONSHIPS

The time is now. The message is urgent: self-directed learning is pivotal to the future — for you, for your family, for the country. How you reach out — and how soon — to self-guide your learning will determine your destiny.

Having just lived through a global pandemic, and still in economic upheaval, civic uproar, unprecedented shifts for college calendars and admission, hastily-crafted online learning for school children, changes in varsity sports commitments — we watch and wonder as we learn quickly and adapt with grace.

Which issues are motivated by politics, subtle or overt? By volatile economics? By health questions, legitimate or otherwise? By civic uproar? Which are topics "whose time had come" but needed a shield to hide behind to shift with less reproach?

Those who step up and meet challenges with inquiry will always be a step ahead.

Our most precious commodity that we complain we never have enough of is time. If we use our time to self-reflect and plan ahead, focusing on committing to our own self-directed learning, we will emerge better and stronger, more assured of our future. Due to unprecedented circumstances, we have been forced to take charge of our own learning, a task we should be doing regardless of world events, something to be strongly aware of right now and in the future. As we are returning to work, to school, to college — it is time to reboot our lives, our processes, our educational system, our priorities.

"Just In Time" Learning

Actually, we should all be life-long learners. "Just in time" learning drives us all — whether we need to find a quick podcast to remind us how to change a flat tire in the middle of the highway, tie a bowtie as we rush out to a big event, or sizzle a steak on the new Green Egg on the porch.

Personally relevant learning happens through self-pursuit. When the gusto comes from within, when we see the purpose and feel the drive for inquiry, for preparation, for pursuit, we have lit the fire within us. It is in the self-pursuit of education that we thrive.

Experiences actually get into the biology of our bodies, laying the foundation for future productivity and health. These experiences shape the people we become. Genes are just the beginning, the first step. Their interaction with the environment will determine individual outcome. In order to develop and function effectively, the prefrontal lobes — the control center of our body — need to be exercised and instructed.

Personal Experiences Shape Brain Architecture

Many think of a brain as a vessel into which we pour knowledge. Actually, our brains function more like a net — constructing a series of electrical connections.

We are born astonishingly unfinished. Specialized cells are in place at birth. Then, the focus shifts to building the connections into a highly integrated system of circuits. Genes provide the cells and put them in place. Experience grows the connections. Then the brain gets rid of what it thinks it will not need, based on its experiences. *Use it or lose it* becomes the imperative.

Think of a fried egg. The white is your cytoplasm. The yolk is the nucleus that contains the master blueprint for your life, your DNA, which carries biological instructions about how tall you will be and how you will respond to stress. Putting DNA into your nucleus is like stuffing 30 miles of fishing line into a blueberry — it's a crowded place! It's not stuffed like cotton in a teddy bear, but rather folded in a complex and tightly regulated manner: molecular origami. Fold one way, it becomes your liver; another way, your bloodstream; another, a nerve cell. Each neuron is an electrically and chemically charged cell.

There is a lightning storm going on in your brain. High voltage! Even if you are feeling lazy or tired, your brain is the busiest and brightest place on the planet. Neurotransmitters — dopamine, serotonin, acetacholine — are the tiny couriers that communicate information across the synaptic cleft. Chemicals release when they are electrically stimulated. These electrical impulses can move at 250 miles per hour — it's a veritable cellular temper tantrum! These electrical and chemical impulses are your brain learning, growing neural pathways.

Meaningful experiences that engage your mind change how your genes are expressed, how your brain grows. Epigenetics — this exchange between genes and environment — shapes the person you will become.

Brain Rules, Medina, J./ *Incognito*, Eagleman, D./ *Live Wires*, Muir, J.

The Apprenticeship Model Is As Old As History Itself

Laws concerning an apprentice go back almost four thousand years ago to the Code of Hammurabi, an ancient Babylonian legal text. The training of a skilled craftsman at the hands of a master workman is an ancient form of the tutorial relationship where the teacher-student ratio is one-to-one.

Clearly, the apprentice system still survives all over the world, and not just among medical interns in hospitals and dedicated student interns in summer theaters. Those in pursuit of self-directed learning seek the mentor who will guide them in their quest.

Many young men and women are in a hurry for a quick return, wanting to be the boss or the entrepreneur straight off; and they would much prefer to "arrive" than to "travel." They do not see a need to float; they want to fly. But for all the bright eyes and eager hands of young people in a hurry, they may not actually be ready to hop straight to the top.

Prudent, self-directed learners face up to the rigorous training required to lead and seek it by finding the connections that will arm them with the experience, knowledge, and wisdom they know they will need. They want to earn what they expect to receive. They have figured out that they must set in place the learning relationships themselves. They must be appropriately assertive — and doggedly persistent.

Apprenticeships have morphed into internships by name, with more relaxed standards than the legal contracts of old. In addition, they have also come under fire as the Department of Labor has intentionally put in place rigorous restrictions to protect student interns from exploitation. Historically, some individuals or companies have sought to profit from those who seek to train under them, without due compensation for their efforts.

The Apprentice's Secret

The word "apprentice" comes from an old French word meaning "to learn — to lay hold of with the mind." This type of learning is the apprentice's secret. With it comes direction, movement forward, hope, and new life. An apprentice is not a person standing still, becoming iced-over, older by the hour. An apprentice sees far horizons. The apprentice's secret is to live life to the fullest because "apprentice" becomes a mindset wrapped around forever learning. All good and happy people are apprentices who will and should remain so to the end of their lives. The purpose of education — whether overtly expressed, left silent or ignored — is to produce apprentices: life-long learners.

We should never assume that a person with a diploma is an educated person, finished with learning. The aim of education, really, is to put the fire of learning in our hearts, knowing that we need to be learning all our days. That is where self-directed learning sets a person apart, assures him a full life — keeps him radiant with inquiry, keeps his brain alive and well. The ongoing mindset of an apprentice will produce abundant life, not internal aging, that death of brain cells of the mind and spirit that comes from accepting the status quo as enough. The self-directed learner knows how to put in a new crop from time to time to preserve the soil and avoid ruinous erosion — to hold on to adventure, hope, wonder.

The Information Explosion On The Digital Landscape

Like it or not, we are all apprentices because we live in the midst of an information explosion on a digital landscape in a world that will always outrun even our keenest minds and the highest level of our competence.

Our Talent May Never Be Quite Enough

We move forward to grow beyond where we are. We seek to measure the distance between what is and what could be. It is up to us. In our world of expanding knowledge, we turn to the experts in moments when we seek to surge forward, to move beyond where we are. There is much within our power, great themes we can isolate and enrich by experience, many breakthroughs we can make with the apprentice's spirit in our hearts. We think of teachers we have supervised who ask for a raise, noting twenty years of service, and we think quietly with angst for the students, "You have not had twenty years' experience; you've had the same experience twenty times."

Beckoning Frontiers

There are still beckoning frontiers in medicine and science, social justice, technology, supply chains, political tone and structure, cleaning the air we breathe, and vexing problems of education. In all these areas, and more, there is healthy ferment with incredible need.

The spirit of the apprentice, always in pursuit of fresh ideas, can become the source of the creative problem solving in such demand. The apprentice's secret is, in fact, not a secret at all — it is a clarion call to action, for self-directed learning! Starting now!!

Internship In Cancer Research

I was in awe about what procedures a research lab must go through in order to get an experimental drug through the FDA. I learned proper procedures in working with lab animals, about the metastisis of cancerous cells, and the removal of tumors. Being a researcher requires a great deal of specialization and even though communication might be rare, every individual in the lab is dependent on the others — such as, if the chemists did not have a chemical prepared for the biological researcher, progress stopped. I witnessed researchers and doctors who are highly dedicated. I know that I want to be part of a group similar to this team because of their attitude: they see their patients as people, not just as cancer victims. I was inspired.

Harvard University – Cambridge, Massachusetts

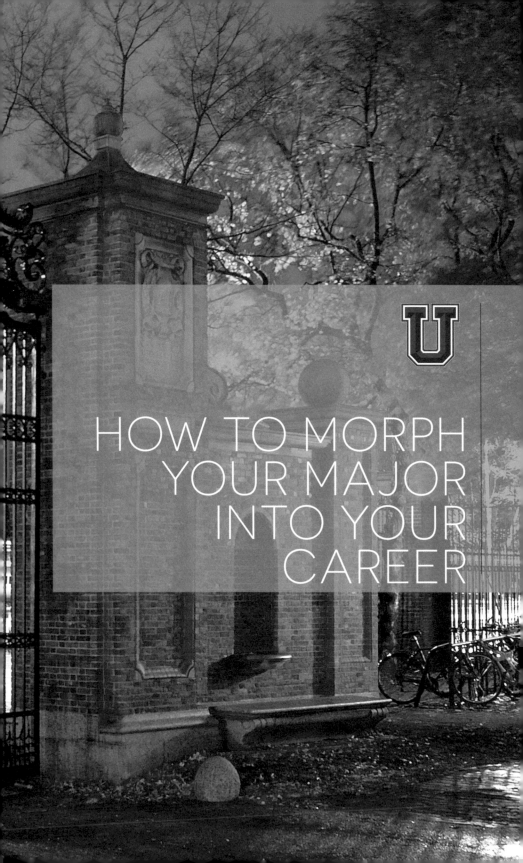

HOW TO MORPH YOUR MAJOR INTO YOUR CAREER

MAJORS, MINORS, AND CERTIFICATES

Think about how you can find areas you want to explore as an apprentice. While the sciences can lead to logical end results such as medicine and research, many courses have creative outlets that are not so obvious. Start by looking into what others have pursued as a career from the major you are investigating, and then get strategic, stretch your thinking, and reach out into the community and start asking questions. You could even harness your family members' creative energy by getting them to ask their friends and associates to help find potential mentors.

What Is A College Major?

Colleges want to know which department you will be spending your time in once you arrive at their school. The concentrated area of study you choose will eventually become your major. Some students know what they want to study before they go to college; some choose once they are on campus; some change their mind — seven times is the national average!

Deciding On Your College Major

When thinking about a major, think about things you like to do and areas you naturally gravitate to and dig into — stories that send you down the internet rabbit hole. Once you establish the subjects you like, you can look into actual majors — which can be organized differently, depending on the school. It is important to think about what classes actually make up a major so you can see the nuances of what exactly you would be studying at each school in a particular area. You can siphon out the words in the program and course descriptions to direct your self-directed learning in pursuing internships that match your projected major.

As you peruse college specific websites, look for the classes that you would take within a major, using the following as an example:

Business majors tend to have classes such as these:
- Accounting
- Entrepreneurship
- Finance
- Hospitality management
- International business
- Management
- Marketing (sometimes can be in communications)

Engineering majors might prioritize the following classes:
- Biomedical
- Chemical
- Computer
- Electrical
- Industrial
- Mechanical

Many schools are now offering interdisciplinary majors, which combine several areas of interest.

Interdisciplinary Majors

While the focus of classes may land in a specific area, there can also be room for taking several electives, even adding a double major, minor, or a certificate in relevant areas of interest.

University of Pennsylvania — Philosophy, Politics, Economics

PPE provides a foundation, including economics, psychology, and ethics so that students can better understand how political and economic systems interact.

Classes:

- Economics Strategic Reasoning
- Public Policy Process
- Behavioral Economics and Psychology

Stanford — Science, Technology, and Society

Provides students with an interdisciplinary framework through which to understand the complex interactions of science, technology and the social world. The major draws on humanities and social sciences approaches to study science and technology in their social context.

Concentrations:

- The Public Life of Science and Technology
- The Future of Information
- Catastrophic Risks and Solutions
- Innovation and Organization
- Life Sciences and Health
- Politics and Policy
- Social Dynamics of Data and Information

Southern Methodist University — Creative Computing

An interdisciplinary major combining theory and methodology from computer science and engineering with aesthetic principles and creative practice from the arts. The program requires students to pursue coursework in both the Lyle School of Engineering and Meadows School of the Arts.

Classes:

- Sound and Code
- Postmodern Software Design
- Digital/Hybrid Media

Claremont McKenna – Integrated Sciences

Scientific Discovery and Innovation present enormous benefits and challenges for society including how we contribute to the health of our species, improve quality of life, drive economic growth, and protect our planet for future generations. This major is based in the liberal arts with a leadership mission. Its approach is to organize a science education around socio-scientific challenges, leveraging computation as a powerful vehicle for discovery and systematic solutions and integrating the social sciences and humanities

Classes:

- The Codes of Life
- Foundations of Leadership
- Moral and Political Issues

Tufts – Engineering Psychology/Human Factors Engineering

Human Factors Engineering (or Engineering Psychology) is an interdisciplinary program offered jointly by the mechanical engineering and psychology departments in either the School of Arts and Sciences or School of Engineering. Engineering psychologists apply knowledge of human behavior to the design of products, equipment, machines, and large-scale systems for human use. Human factors engineers apply principles of psychology and engineering to design medical devices, evaluate software interfaces, or set product safety standards.

Classes:

- Introduction to Human Factors
- Ergonomics Human
- Machine System Design
- Fuzzy Sets and Genetic Algorithms

Duke

Interdepartmental major, choose and combine two areas of your choice.

University of Texas at Austin

Offers Minors and Certificate Programs in areas from Ethics & Leadership in Business to Digital Humanities to Creative Writing.

What You Learn From Others

People have morphed arts/business/engineering/neuroscience/global initiatives into personally relevant and personally satisfying careers, such as the following:

Intern at Investment Firm

I discovered that table etiquette and attire could make or break a business deal. I learned when to wear a tie, which fork to use for my salad, and where to put my napkin at dinners with prospective clients.

Intern at NASA

I spent time observing, tracking, cataloging, and analyzing "orbital debris" — fragments of broken-up satellites and rocket bodies that pollute our orbital atmosphere. My duties included screening video data taken from telescopes, looking for and cataloging satellites and meteors, and writing a program to derive plate scale and position angle corrections factors for our video sensors. While these tasks were initially foreign and complicated to me, I quickly grew comfortable with the people, the jargon, and the work. I found active scientific research exhilarating in that I was able to accomplish something new. I was not just following the lab instruction sheet from a school textbook. Here, at the edge of man's knowledge, the search required a slow, methodical progression from one absolute truth to another. Watching the minds of many of the nations' top astronomers at work was a thrill. Lunch discussions included shop-talk on the ultimate fate of the universe. If I were to become a co-scientist in future national endeavors, I realized I would be applying every brain cell I have to help hammer out new data or play with new ideas!

Intern at International Law Firm, Barcelona

It was absolutely essential that I make a good impression, since navigating Barcelona's labyrinthine public transportation system rendered me late to my first meeting. I had flown 4000 miles to attend a conference with lawyers from around the globe who sought to create an international law firm, and I did not want to miss a minute of the action. The meetings were held mostly in French, so I spent several hours translating for my American mentor. I began to realize how very important my fluency in three foreign languages can be. The possibilities for a future career in international law raced through my mind. Many translations, research projects, and summary reports of government releases later, I realized that the legal profession held a potential career match for me.

Intern at Real Estate Development Company

I learned that staying informed leads to sound business decisions - so I started each day with news updates. I also learned that cooperation within an industry is vital for success, that innovation distinguishes projects, that working as a team matters to employers, and that the business world is a tough place to survive. Most importantly, I learned that one must honor his word and be trustworthy.

Intern at Petroleum Engineering Company

Before this internship, I wanted to be a petroleum engineer because I thought it would be fun – like being a modern-day treasure hunter. Afterwards, I realized that understanding the energy industry was a moral responsibility for me to help the United States economy become stable by being less dependent on foreign energy.

London School of Economics – London, England

MAKING YOUR
EDUCATION
RELEVANT

MAJORS ARE MERELY A PLACE TO START

A college major is merely a place to start thinking about and preparing for a future career path. Many majors can become foundational for a range of professional options. Numerous fields offer transferable skills across a range of employment tracks. Be creative. Reach out. Think broadly. Have fun pursuing options.

Remember, also, that success comes from more than what you will learn in your classes. An internship can help distinguish you for both your admission to college and also for a future job application. An internship can last a day, a week, a summer, or a semester — whatever time frame works for you and for your sponsor. Some internships might be project or research-based; others might have to be "job shadowing" to appease the parameters of Human Resource Departments and to comply with federal mandates about avoiding exploitation.

Strategic planning for appropriate internships requires that you scrutinize your interests and aptitudes. Internships provide a vehicle for learning about the global marketplace you will enter, building a network in the business community, thinking about potential college majors and future career paths, securing an additional letter of recommendation from someone who will know you in a different context, and — most importantly — learning about yourself. Experience shapes your journey. Experience crafts your story. Experience molds you and unleashes your potential.

The match of intern and mentor defines the depth of your learning and the impact the experience will have on your future. It is the understanding that you gain and the story you can tell about the work you did — not the name of the organization on the neon sign — that will capture the attention of the admission officer or future employer. These are the components of your well-crafted resume in which you quantify the details of your experience and contribution.

Internships invite you to interact with your world. Be appropriately aggressive and sleuth out the opportunities that await you. Create your own experiences. Using initiative to find a good internship is a growth experience in itself. Push out the walls of your classrooms and stretch your learning.

Get ready to tie your academic work and personal experiences together to secure your future. Keep reading to figure out HOW to present yourself and connect with the world beyond college!

Day One Or One Day

High school and college offer shiny diplomas, but they do not tell what you have learned, describe your skill sets, or reveal your character. There are emerging and multiple ways to grow the connective tissue between an academic profile, personal credentials, and an application. Students find a major; then, they need to know how to apply that degree to land a position. Success comes from more than textbook knowledge.

Experiences, internships, relationships, personalized learning can shape future aspirations and provide the fodder and the skillsets beyond the academic foundations needed to get the nod.

What employers want and the hiring process they use to decide whom to hire is often inefficient. They are concerned about having employees stay, be part of a team, and be productive. What these new employees do will help build — or compromise — their company's brand.

It is important to remember that both colleges during admission cycles and employers during hiring seasons are looking for evidence of intellectual curiosity, initiative, and leadership; they are trying to decipher how you will enrich their communities. Colleges are looking for predictors of how you might use the degree they are bestowing upon you as a change-agent in the world to enhance their rankings. Employers are sleuthing out indicators that you can help them build their bank accounts. Institutional agendas — both academic and corporate — can change, from year to year, making the process more complicated, highly nuanced, and less transparent.

Most colleges see their purpose as teaching students to be employable over their lifetime. Yet, colleges do not always teach the immediate skill sets that employers want new hires to start with on their first day. Few colleges prepare their graduates to enter the marketplace ready to add value and relevance beyond crunching the numbers.

So, you must be strategic as you present yourself and seek life beyond college!

The following pages showcase possible college majors as well as job opportunities that may emerge from courses you may choose to focus on in college. Also included in this section — and throughout the text — are excerpts from what student interns have shared with us as they completed their programs with personally-matched mentors. Their honest appreciation, remarkable awareness, and personal growth astound us and reinforce repeatedly the impact of engaging with mentors who care. Their insights filled us with awe, and they became an inspiration for this part of the book.

BIOCHEMISTRY

Physician
Researcher
Scientist
Pharmaceutical Company
Hospital Administration
Dentist
Surgical Technician

Software Developer
Quality Control Analyst
Nurse
Physician's Assistant
Chemist
Pharmacist
Clinical Research

Surgery

I peered at the carefully arranged array of tools and materials on the table before me, wondering how so many different items are required for just one surgery. Minutes later, I watched the scalpel trace a thin line down the patient's sternum. After a few deft maneuvers by the surgeon, I gazed upon the beating heart of another human being. Observing open-heart surgery for the first time was definitely one of the most memorable things I have done in my life. With every procedure I watched, I was constantly blown away by the miracle of modern medicine and how it is possible to open a human being up like the hood of a car to make repairs.

Children's Hospital

I read *Comprehensive Surgical Management of Congenital Heart Disease* to learn about basic heart anatomy so I could understand what normally happens before beginning to tackle complex defects and their surgical repairs. Whenever I read or heard a new vocabulary word, I looked it up in Wikipedia so I could understand the surgery I would see each day. I learned about deoxygenated blood flow, the superior and inferior vena cavas, tricuspid valves, pulmonary artery, mitral valve, arterial switch procedure to correct a dextrotransposition of the great arteries, and Tetralogy of Fallot — another congenital disease. The first day in the operating room I was clueless, but with the help of the textbook, I began to understand and be in awe of the daily procedures and the remarkable medical team that performed life-saving surgeries.

BUSINESS/ ECONOMICS

Accounting
Banking
Retail Companies
Financial Planning

Government Agencies
Investment Firms
Non-profit Organizations
Researcher and Forecaster

Finance

I studied the process of trading stock, bonds, and options. My days started at 5:30 a.m. so I could be included in the morning conference calls and Zoom meetings where analysts make their daily forecasts. The frenetic pace included focused research for portfolio reviews, daily awareness of the news that could affect the market, and frequent interaction with brokers calling in with questions. At my fingertips I had the latest in market technology, including data analytics and the most accurate resources; in addition, I had opportunities to interact with leaders in the economic field. This experience prepared me to make an informed decision as I pursued career options.

Global Insurance Company, London

I developed a basic understanding of shipping, which facilitated my understanding of the insurance industry. I accompanied brokers who insure risks with oil and gas in the North Sea, as well as marine brokers who insure ships and their agents. I learned the polar side of insurance. Brokers often are apt to make a risk sound as safe as possible, while underwriters search deeply for flaws in a given risk, such as a five-year loss record. Finally, I worked with the teams responsible for writing the policies and making the market-going brokers understand the risks they were trying to insure. This part of the business is highly technical and requires a certain penchant for detail. I was able to pick up relatively involved knowledge of insurance that I, otherwise, would not have been able to procure. I thoroughly enjoyed my tenure in London, having enjoyed the city and its people as much as my job, making me think deeply about a career in a global market and, potentially, living abroad.

ENGINEERING

Software Engineer

Petroleum Companies

City Planner

Bio Researcher

Naval Testing Facility

The first part of my work was with a mechanical engineer who taught me to use a computer program that enabled me to reverse engineer an instrumentation board that needed to be put into a palette for an F-18 aircraft. This program was amazing — efficient and fast. But most of my time I spent in the hangar or on the flight line. I got to sit in four different aircraft and load software onto their systems. The only way to do this is to power up the plane, turn on the avionics and other instruments, and load it from the cockpit. I got to sit in the cockpit and turn on the switches and push the different buttons. I actually sat alone in an F-18 cockpit that was fueled and ready for take-off. In addition, I changed the video recorders located behind the ejection seat. This task really scared me because in order to reach the equipment, I had to maneuver into the area behind the seat where the explosives were located that could blow open the canopy to release the ejection seat. While I was in the hangar, I removed and added various kinds of equipment from the aircraft, work which became somewhat routine after a few days. I learned a great deal about engineering, security, and fighter planes. I could see how important the nuances of engineering and technology would be in making my future decisions about a career.

Energy

I discovered the process for finding oil and natural gas is very complicated. I learned about what multiple natural phenomena make drilling a reservoir optimal, about different methods of coring and drilling, about the appearance of salt domes and their effect on reservoirs they pass through, the advantages of sidewall coring, the difficulty with directional drilling and about running a successful business. I learned a lot about this industry.

ENGLISH

Writer
Marketing and Sales
Public Relations Firm
Journalist

Copy Editor
Advertising Firm
Content Producer
Novelist

Video Production

I was invited to go on a shoot in the videomobile. I helped the crew set up the lights, the microphones and the cables. When the director started yelling instructions at the cameraman, I knew this was real. I had no idea how much was involved in taping a television show. I managed to keep my spot on the crew for taping various shows. I usually worked the camera, but a couple of times I was the floor director and worked audio and lights. The first time I worked the camera, I have to admit I was a little nervous. My hands sweated throughout the program as I received instructions from my headset. In my spare time I was shown how to edit, how to work the digital effects, and how to work a character generator. I made several promos. Now that I know how special effects are done, my way of "seeing" programs and ads is enhanced forever. This experience provided a great beginning education for what I would like to do in the future.

Education

I've discovered that when a place feels nurturing, safe, and supportive, it's the perfect environment for learning. I believe that reassurance is what makes students strive to be their best. I think devoting your time to working with children is a selfless job. It's making your life all about making other lives stand out and grow.

Museum

I came away with a much better understanding of the unnoticed labor that goes behind each museum exhibit, as well as with an increased interest in marketing and sales in the art industry.

HISTORY

College Professor
Teacher
Museum Curator
Attorney
Government Office
Politician

Researcher
Ambassador
Librarian
US State Department
Foreign Affairs Analyst
Archivist

Museum Of Natural Science

I was entranced standing under something that was hundreds of millions of years older than I was. I touched these dinosaurs with my own two hands. I was asked to climb into the T-Rex exhibit and glue a number to its foot — the task represented far more to me than "keeping all the artifacts in order."

Archaeological Exploration

Through excavation to discover the prehistoric societies of Mallorca, I was intrigued with history whenever I found pieces of angora jars or Roman nails. Though each member of my team was a distinct individual, I found us united in our finds, songs, and patience. When we excavated, our ages did not matter; but our interest and enthusiasm in our work and in each other did. An unforgettable experience that guided my direction for my future career path, pulling on my fascination with historical detail.

European Decorative Arts Museum

I experienced the visceral effects of art and its ability to inextricably touch a viewer's soul. I learned about paintings and sculptures, as well as furniture and decorative objects, and also about the day-to-day life of a museum curator. I contributed posts for the museum blogs that focused on historic modes of interior design. I loved seeing the beautiful, immaculately furnished house and the behind-the-scenes-goings-on in the offices. I learned the intricacies of putting together exhibits and how much research goes into creating them. I learned right away that the educational focus of a museum is equally as important as the curatorial side to make the art more accessible to people. I now know that I want to work in a museum surrounded by all the decorative arts that inspire me.

MARKETING/ COMMUNICATIONS/ PUBLIC RELATIONS

Advertising Agencies	Service Industries
Public Relations	Political Campaigns
Department Stores	Insurance Agencies

Entertainment

While I sorted through piles of fan mail and lifted shipments of soda cans, I also learned the factors that go into a truly incredible script, how to create an acting reel and how to read character breakdowns. I now know how certain actions translate on camera. I also made valuable friendships, mastered how to load a stapler, and how to fix a printer. I had a wonderful experience, translating this industry to meet my future goals.

Fashion Magazine, New York City

Though fascinated with the fashion industry, I was not sure I was cut out for the intense, diehard world of fashion journalism. Yet, my time at the magazine unfolded with a litany of interesting (and, yes, at times monotonous) tasks. I hopped from fashion editors, to features editors, to photo researchers, to "style bloggers." My projects ranged from organizing photographs from runway shows and writing cutlines to calling Hollywood stylists to figure out who's wearing what. This experience confirmed that I could thrive in this profession and reaffirmed my commitment to journalism, whether fashion or otherwise.

Congressional Office

I learned about the importance of correspondence with a politician's constituents. I realized the significance of public opinion and accessibility of elected state officials to assure a reliable means for staying connected regarding pivotal issues. I am definitely a more educated voter.

PHILOSOPHY

Teacher

Private Equity

Admissions Counselor

College President

Marketing Director

FBI

District Attorney

Web Analyst

Software Developer

Editor

Conservationist

Attorney

Criminal District Courts

I saw plea deals ranging from stealing lingerie at Walmart to identity theft and trials ranging from juvenile misdemeanors to capital murders.

Wildlife Biologist

In the 1870's, hunters in the Yellowstone area poisoned wolves for their hides. By 1930, wolves no longer existed in the park. By now, people have worked to bring the wolf back and study the impact in an attempt to balance this significant ecosystem in the temperate zone, especially on the elk, one of a wolf's main food sources. My objective was to find out the land use patterns of elk. I began at 6:30 each morning, collecting statistics: habitat type, food availability, slope, elevation, snow characteristics. I recorded tracks and observed wildlife. The days were hard, freezing, and long — but well worth the struggle endured. I saw that any change brings controversy and requires diligent documentation. I learned how challenging it is to lead a wildlife research project, but I could see how rewarding the work of wildlife biology could feel and how great it is to be in the great outdoors from day to day!

Environmentalist

I never knew that turtles had claws on their flippers, nor how fragile hatching turtles are. I analyzed sea turtle gut contents to identify their feeding grounds. This was tedious and monotonous, but very interesting: crab appendages, fish bones, tubeworms, maggots. I formed many environmental theories as I observed. I will continue to research my hypotheses in the future as a wildlife biologist.

POLITICAL SCIENCE

Attorney
City or Town Management
Law Enforcement
School Districts
Federal/Local Government
Foreign Service

Elected Leadership
Political Advising
Consulting Firms
Public Administration
Politician
Courts

Congressional Office
Washington, DC

My main jobs were to answer the mail and pick up the phones to help make the office run more efficiently. I saw the power of lobbyists and interest groups; mail poured in daily representing oil companies, health care advocacy groups, foreign investors. I read correspondence trying to influence new legislation. Most important was the constituent mail; people either strongly agreed with or clearly questioned the Congressman's policies. I realized that diversity of opinion means that some will inevitably be unhappy, regardless of legislative results. I also attended briefings and meetings on issues from foreign and diplomatic security policy to projections on the economy. I have a new awareness of the stressors for Congressional leaders who are trying to research, listen to divergent perspectives, and create workable solutions. I am determined to be a future voice in our government, one who listens carefully and works hard to promote reasonable compromise.

Courtrooms

My time in the criminal, civil, juvenile and federal courtrooms clarified how society deals with legal issues which people encounter on a daily basis and how the legal system resolves these human issues within the parameters of law and order. This experience confirmed my decision to become a lawyer.

The White House
Washington, DC

How incredible to be in the center of a massive transition in political power. Emotions ran wild as Presidential appointees packed their last boxes to end an era in political history. Answering the phones was one of my main jobs; during my hundred plus calls per day, I spoke with congressmen, governors, cabinet members, and famous celebrities. Amazingly, reading the mail was one of the best ways I learned about the job of the Department of Political Affairs; I read everything from environmental and economic bills to pledges and proposals to make the United States a better nation. As I went to the south lawn of the White House to see the President take off for his last trip to Camp David, I was touched by the Presidential staff's cheering and waving flags and banners. I remember the loud hum of the propellers and the strong gust of wind as the helicopter took off; but what I remember most were the tears. I felt, again, the end of an era of service. As I walked down the steps for the last time into the dark, cold Washington night, I began to cry. I cried for all the wonderful people I had met who would no longer have a job; I cried for the great man who was leaving his post; I cried because I sensed an emotional moment of change in history. I knew I would need to find my own place in the continuing history of our nation.

Federal District Court

I observed court proceedings, probable cause hearings, plea bargains, jury selections, and trials that dealt with drugs, assaults, and thefts. Accompanying a Judge to an inner-city elementary school where he talked to students about making wise choices, I was sad to see children who hear gunshots and watch drug deals on the way to school. I toured holding cells, jails where convicted felons are incarcerated, and the lethal injection chamber at the death house. A particularly meaningful moment came at the graduation ceremony for a bootcamp for Class C felons, aging from 17 to 26 years old. My experience helped me realize that I want to be a prosecutor. I am committed to trying to help people make better choices - and to protecting those who become victims.

PSYCHOLOGY

Counselor
Human Resources
Client Services
Physical Therapist

School Psychologist
Therapist
Behavior Technician
Nutritionist

Therapeutic Interventions

I observed and learned about children who are in pain. The first few days were difficult; I was exhausted. I met with doctors, therapists, and psychological technicians to discuss the certain behavioral patterns and why these children could not function in a normal classroom environment. In many cases, this center was the only secure and stable place for these children who had faced personal violence at such a young age. Within each of these children, I found a yearning for security and love that I wanted to fulfill. As a result of my work, I understand how to look at young children with more empathy and understanding.

Hospital

The time I spent revealed the complex network of team players that harmonize to form a community of caretakers who aim to serve and to heal. Standing no more than four feet away from a patient, I witnessed the pages of my textbook come alive, jump out, find new meaning. From neurosurgery and craniotomies, to plastic surgery and abdominoplasty – I was able observe a pastiche of specialties and procedures, determining what I want to do in the future. Thanks to the supportive and friendly cast of nurses, doctors, and educators, I do not have to wait for my third year of medical school to experiment with different concentrations. I have identified orthopedics as the target for my professional career.

Nutritionist

Working in Preventive Medicine reinforced the importance of a healthy diet. I realized how much I had taken for granted and became sensitive to areas of nutrition and conscientious reading of labels. I got heart-healthy recipes and tried many of them. I realized that the health profession is not an easy field to be a part of and that those individuals who work to save and aid the lives of others certainly deserve a tremendous amount of praise and respect. I am committed to working in this field in the future.

SOCIOLOGY

Politician
Researcher
Family Therapist
Social Worker
Non-profit companies

Hospital Case Worker
Peace Corps
Psychologist
Archaeologist
Client Services

Orphanage

I had made the assumption that girls who had been abandoned would accept love and compassion. But what I learned was that they sometimes build walls around their hearts in self-defense and have a hard time trusting others. I experienced charity in which you get nothing in return — often no gratitude or appreciation. But you keep on loving and helping anyway because you know they need it.

Nursing

In each operating room I watched surgeons as they skillfully operated on the body's most vital organs and realized the responsibility that comes with entering the medical field. I was in awe as I observed a coronary artery bypass. I learned procedures required for cardiovascular, neurological, hand, ear, nose, and throat problems; the importance of the sterile field; the necessity of dedication and excellence; the emotional side of medicine, as well. I also realized the gratitude we owe to nurses. While most of us give due respect to surgeons, we can easily forget the dedication and effort put forth by nurses who deal with both sides of the surgical procedure: the emotional and the physical. They comfort and scrub; they hold hands and hand instruments. Often nurses know just about as much about surgical procedures as surgeons themselves do. The surgeons and nurses work as one body, synchronizing to perfection through years of practice. Watching these people do the work they love gave me inspiration.

THEATER/ DANCE STUDIO ART

Photography Studio
Teacher
Theater Company
Reporter
Talent Agency
Production Companies
Artist

Cruise Lines
Theme Parks
Resorts
Television/Movie
Studios
Graphic Designer

Singer
Music/Art Therapist
Blogger
Voice Coach
Museum Director
Event Planning

Graphic Design

I studied editorial cartoon anthologies and syndicated cartoons. I observed worthwhile techniques and "tricks of the trade." I learned about controversy over editorial cartooning from study and discussion — about whether or not cartoonists sell out to a chance for awards and money when they accept edgy assignments, potentially laced with political innuendo. I learned not only how to produce an editorial cartoon, but — more importantly — the philosophy behind editorial cartooning with its professional wit and whimsy, and — perhaps — its opportunity to contribute to a better world, if one is visionary. I am considering a variation of this field as a career option.

Professional Artist

I saw how an artist works, not just how he paints. The urge and desire to paint are always present, and the inspiration that morphs into a painting may strike at any time. Art can be a waiting game and a thinking game — waiting for an idea to leap from obscurity to clarity, then thinking of the most effective way to make the idea take physical shape on a canvas. An artist has no fixed hours and, unfortunately, no fixed income. Behind the romance and mystery of the world of art, dealers and collectors buy, sell, and manipulate the business; sometimes, the art might take a back seat to politics and money matters. Working under a professional artist is the true way for a newcomer to learn the ropes of the art world. I now have an even greater interest in becoming a professional, fine artist than ever before.

URBAN STUDIES

Marketing and Events	City Planner
Real Estate	Civil Engineer
Non-Profit company	Government Employee

Architecture

I dug into SketchUp and AutoCAD, learning keyboard shortcuts and new commands as quickly as possible so I could transfer designs onto SketchUp. I realized that architecture would be a perfect match for me.

Public Relations Office, Costa Rica

In addition to speaking Spanish and working in public relations, I discovered a new culture: its economy, land, people, and family life. Outside of my long days in the office, I marveled at the beaches covered with risen coral due to a recent earthquake, and drove quickly through the rain forests on my daily commute to avoid the frequent landslides resulting from intense humidity and frequent rain that often block transportation. I learned about banana plants and coffee beans. I returned with more knowledge about public relations, more fluency in Spanish, an awareness of a new culture, and the desire to explore more countries all over the world. Thanks for this amazing experience. PURA VIDA!

NASA, Houston

The big test was to verify proper performance of the primary life support system, which is the space suit that the astronauts wear, at vacuum in a manned chamber run. My assignment was to record the systems as they were powered up and taken offline so that later NASA could go back and see how long the suit was running on its own power and how efficiently the suit was functioning. Aside from the vacuum test, I was able to tour the mock-up shuttle and space station used for training plus the other test chambers. I was able to meet lots of people and ask lots of questions — about how things work/react in space, about the astronauts and their life in the space station, about the future of NASA and — most importantly — how I could become an astronaut.

(And, a few years later, he DID become an astronaut!)

Yale University – New Haven, Connecticut

PRESENTING THE AUTHENTIC U

INTRODUCING YOURSELF

There are still high standards in this anything-goes-world for some things, and college admissions and job offers are two of them. How you present yourself and your story really matters. There is an effective way to communicate from your initial call to your interview to your thank you note. Keep reading to make sure you set yourself up for success.

You Have One Chance To Make A First Impression

Graduates can write a research paper — but not necessarily an email, one that is short, concise, and asks a well-phrased question for a job interview without offending someone. These pivotal emails often lack specificity and emotion; students have been graded on content, not presentation. Graduates historically have done projects with little opportunity to apply feedback, to modify content, and redo for improvement. This lack of practice risks having new employees unable to accept negative feedback on the job site — a trait employers are hoping to avoid, a communication deficit that can be costly in seeking the nod from a potential employer. Companies want employees that are coachable and willing to learn from mistakes without meltdowns.

Emotional Intelligence Matters

Both college admission deans and human resource personnel are looking for emotional intelligence — applicants who can recognize and understand the emotions of others and adjust their own accordingly in order to build a positive and productive relationship. The ability to control and manage one's own emotions and to handle interpersonal relationships judiciously and empathetically are predictors of positive outcomes for any group adding new people. Gatekeepers are seeking newcomers with the ability to express their own thoughts and feelings while simultaneously adjusting to the thoughts and feelings of others.

The Best Fit

Many high school seniors apply to the Ivies because they think they are supposed to. Yet, we have had students turn down prestigious, top-ranked colleges because they discovered that these schools did not offer the deep-level programs relevant to the majors they needed to succeed in their career goals. High school seniors have come to measure their worth by the colleges to which they apply and college graduates, by the companies which grant them an interview. This mindset blurs their vision. Their identity gets wrapped up in the name of the school or the company, bypassing whether or not that school or industry is their best fit. They get tied up in the image, the perceived prestige. This blurred mindset can slip forward into job applications beyond college applications. Remember to hold on to the goal of finding the best fit whether college or career, beyond the best name brand.

Beyond Academics

Internships, beyond academic programs, often give students the courage to make the right choice for their future. There is more than the brand name that needs to go into a final decision about which college to attend or which company to work for. Going through internship experiences can reveal what might be the best personal program, guiding an applicant to end up in the right place, the happier place, with the best fit.

Today, students are drawn to the brand of the Ivies — perceiving them to provide a head start in the marketplace because people assume as graduates, they are smart. Some businesses recruit from highly selective colleges because they feel their work has been done for them four years earlier by admission officers who have already vetted the upcoming workforce. Others rely on the flagship state universities, anticipating that their graduates arrive more industry-ready from majors more relevant to the world their graduates will enter.

Become The Best Version Of Yourself

Yet, as Malcolm Gladwell and other researchers have demonstrated, you can be successful regardless of where you start! Ultimately, wherever you land, it is up to you to make the opportunity yours. So, there is no wrong decision. You can become the best version of yourself wherever you land, if you want it badly enough.

Intern in Medical Research

I have done a wide variety of tasks: 'splitting cells;' running DNA gel electrophoresis; working with plasmid DNE — cutting out a length of base pairs of nucleotides, which make up a protein that causes cancer, and replacing it with an insert that would insure that the sequence of nucleotides which made that protein would stop replicating.

Intern in Marine Science

I was part of a team that monitors the songs, migration patterns and diving activity of the humpback whale. Oddly enough, the fluke of a whale is much like our fingerprint; every whale has a unique fluke. The awesome sight of a whale performing a full breach, lifting itself entirely out of the water, was stunning – especially considering these animals can weigh up to 50 tons and reach up to 50 feet long. Projects like these would be an exciting part of my future as a marine scientist!

Focus on the following as you set out to make a first impression.
- Do it right! Get started today.
- Find your strengths.
- Do you work hard and possess a great deal of stamina?
- Do you make things happen by turning thoughts into actions?
- Can you take things as they come and discover the future, one day at a time?
- Do you have the ability to think about the range of factors that might affect a situation?
- Do you have the ability to determine how pieces and resources can be arranged for maximum productivity?
- Can you generally put thoughts into words — yours and others?

Self-reflection can connect you to your personal strengths and help you articulate what matters to you. More clarity can lead to more options.

Increase your awareness, build your network, and let your curiosity or special talent lead you to a career discovery so you are ready to connect through a meaningful first impression.

Yet even when everything about you screams "Hire me!" you'll still need a cover letter to introduce yourself, a resume that gets you noticed, and an interview that connects you.

Get ready. Your time is now. The following will suggest how.

How To Present Yourself

Two documents lead the way to a position, whether as an intern, a summer employee, or for a permanent position: a cover letter and a resume.

The cover letter allows you to tailor your message and introduce yourself. This document gives you a chance to reveal what you have become by the experiences you have had, to translate what has inspired you and what has shaped your aspirations that led you to this particular portal for your next stop. Then, your resume offers details about your education, experiences, and special interests that have led you to apply for this specific position.

Cover Letter

You are seeking your reader's attention to read your resume, to garner an interview, and — ultimately — to get the nod for a position.

A cover letter lets your audience hear your voice. They will see your communication skills, your attention to detail, your intellect, your enthusiasm and your interest in their organization. Your letter should reveal the initiative you have taken to research their programs and goals.

This introduction also offers you a chance to highlight your most significant accomplishments that are most relevant to the position you are seeking.

Your cover letter should be in paragraph form with a conversational tone.

Your opening paragraph should identify the position for which you are applying, show how you learned about it, indicate specific qualifications that would make you a good fit, and suggest why you want to work there.

In the next paragraphs you could quantify relevant experiences or training you have had that qualify you for the position you are seeking beyond details that might appear in your resume. You could feature specific examples that manifest how you have used your talents or skills and share the outcome. Do be careful to avoid having your cover letter morph into a prose version of your resume. Know when to stop.

You could conclude with an action statement — requesting an interview, if appropriate, or a time to meet to supply further information if needed.

Be sure to thank your reader for their consideration of your request.

Resume

Your contact information should be at the top of your resume: name, address, phone, email, web site address — if you have one and if relevant and appropriate.

List educational information, starting with the most recent first.

Next, each experience you list should include a brief description that names your responsibilities; quantifies what skills you used; indicates how many you served; and details your accomplishments. Use action verbs and power words. Many resumes are now reviewed first by artificial intelligence — so the words you use matter in garnering the "hits" that can land you the nod you are seeking. Include name of organization or program, location, title of your position, dates.

You can include sections on special skills, leadership, or athletics.

Proofread carefully to confirm correct spelling. In general, keep to one page, with font size 12 point if possible for spacing, and visually comfortable margins.

You can use creative and descriptive titles for each section of experiences to offer guided reading and suggest your significant distinguishers. You can have different versions of your resume, featuring your accomplishments most relevant to the position you are seeking.

Alert: many readers review a resume in under a minute, so make sure you feature the message you hope to convey through your titles and format.

Interview

Interviews come in many forms.

Personal interviews offer a chance for all parties to meet to determine a good fit for a position. Arrive early. Be courteous to everyone you meet. Be aware of body language. Let the interviewers know what you can do for their program or organization.

Virtual interviews are the new normal. They have their advantages; they can save travel time and expense. They also have their challenges. Be thoughtful about your background. Consider a virtual backdrop, if necessary. Wear appropriate attire. Maintain eye contact. User names matter. If life happens and interrupts, roll with it. Muting can be useful to keep potential distractions in check; use it if you might anticipate a dog barking or a child shrieking. Write out your talking points and practice them in front of a camera. Convey energy. Keep your notes handy. Smile early and often. Be sure the camera lens is at least as high as your head; you can use a stack of books under your laptown to elevate the screen. Keep an appropriate distance from the screen to avoid a wide-angle effect that can distort your facial features.

The best way to prepare for an interview is first to pause and self-reflect. Know yourself. Be able to articulate your past accomplishments, what matters to you, and why you are interested in the position.

Research the field and the particular organization with which you will be connecting. Be aware of leaders and trends in the field, salary ranges, company publications, competition within the trade, challenges within the organization. Prepare questions you might want to ask. Be an active listener. Do not try to dominate the conversation. Think in advance of three points you would like to leave your interviewer with that show your qualifications for the position you are seeking.

You could get open-ended questions that simply ask you to tell the interviewers about yourself or why should they hire you, or you could get behavioral questions that help them explore your soft skills such as character, showing how you would act in hypothetical situations: for example, tell us about a time you set a goal and met it or how you convinced someone to see a situation differently.

At the conclusion of your interview, stress why you are interested in the position and be sure to thank your interviewer for meeting with you. Then send a follow-up email or letter, as an official note of appreciation.

Regardless, enjoy the chance to talk about your proudest moments.

Thank You Note

Make sure to email a thank you note to each person you connect with who makes an effort to help you along the way. Make it thoughtful and appreciative, perhaps including a reference to part of your conversation or something specific you discovered or encountered following your discussion. You might mention you hope to see them again, if appropriate.

An email works well because it will go into your digital file and can be referenced easily through a search. Make sure to add a signature line with your contact information, including your phone number and email address for quick reference.

Thoughtfully-crafted thank you notes are always worthwhile and appreciated.

From An Intern

THANK YOU. Before I even go into what I have just completed, I just want to say that this is one of the most unique and rewarding experiences I have had to date — one that has nudged me to be introspective and deeply thoughtful about the direction I should head in the future, making my decision based on facts, not merely hype. THANK YOU for leading me to these mentoring moments that will shape my future productivity and happiness!

Princeton University – Princeton, New Jersey

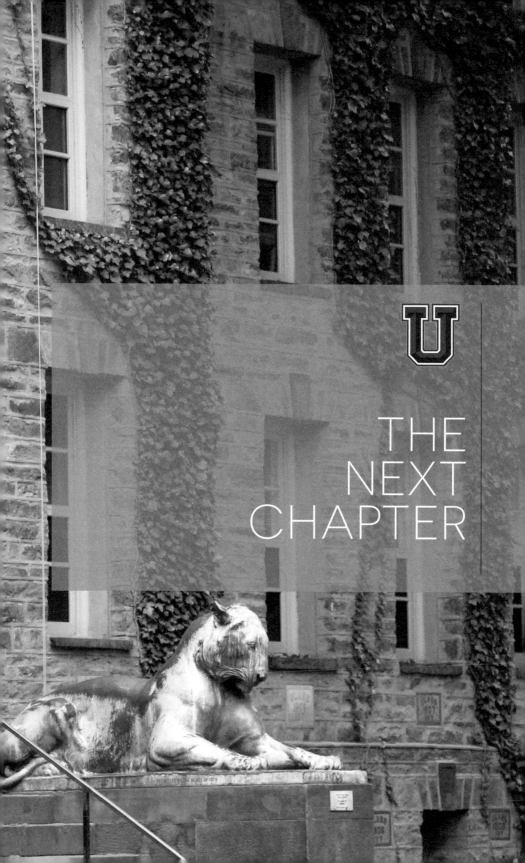

THE
NEXT
CHAPTER

EPILOGUE

E ducation opens minds and leads to solutions. Everyone can learn —
whether vicariously, virtually, or in real time with real people. What
you pursue and what you do with what you learn is, inherently, up
to you. Learning, then, is your responsibility.

You can expand and enrich your education, going beyond your academic
training at school, through self-directed learning — beginning by
connecting with potential mentors. Staying open to guidance is always
productive.

In essence, you are an independent decision maker; it is your responsibility
to take charge and grow. The world does not come to you; you must step
up and reach out to propel your life forward. Self-directed learning can
help you SOAR!

Remember Grandpa John Muir? Recall his authenticity, his directness, and
his well-written and succinct letter. Professionalism matters, even when
you are still in high school. Distinguish yourself, show that you are well-
educated and know what the world is expecting from you.

Investigate, explore profusely, be full of intellectual curiosity, build
relationships, and muster the initiative to do something remarkably
productive, meaningful, and relevant.

The world needs creative problem solvers. The world needs you. Now.

University of Oxford – Oxford, England

LESSONS FROM GEESE

by Milton Olson

1. As each bird flaps its wings, it creates an "uplift" for the bird following. By flying in a "V" formation, the whole flock adds 71% greater flying range than if the bird flew alone.

Lesson: People who share a common direction and sense of community can get where they are going quicker and easier because they are traveling on the thrust of one another.

2. Whenever a goose falls out of formation, it suddenly feels the drag and resistance of trying to fly alone and quickly gets back into formation to take advantage of the "lifting power" of the bird immediately in front.

Lesson: If we have as much sense as a goose, we will stay in formation with those who are headed where we want to go (and be willing to accept their help, as well as give ours to the others).

3. When the lead goose gets tired, it rotates back into the formation and another goose flies to the point position.

Lesson: It pays to take turns doing the hard tasks and sharing leadership with people. As with geese, we are interdependent on each other.

4. The geese in formation honk from behind to encourage those up front to keep up their speed.

Lesson: We need to make sure our "honking" from behind is encouraging — not something else.

5. When a goose gets sick or wounded or shot down, two geese drop out of formation and follow it down to help and protect it. They stay with it until it is able to fly again or dies. Then they launch out on their own, with another formation, or catch up with the flock.

Lesson: If we have as much sense as geese, we-too-will stand by each other in difficult times, as well as when we are strong.

AFTERWORD

University of Oxford – Oxford, England

WITH APPRECIATION

On our journey through education, college admissions, and preparing for career pursuits with well over 5,000 students by now, we have seen first-hand that doing everything the same old way does not serve today's students. Yet, by hopping on the digital train too quickly and too completely, some deeply important ideas and practices that have anchored past generations can become lost.

Perhaps one of the most impactful visionaries we connect with is **Todd Rose**, currently a professor at **Harvard**, and his book, *The End of Average*, which keeps our focus on the variability in our classrooms, reminding us how important it is that we remember that growth is a jagged line, seldom linear, and that we can meet our students where they are and give them what they need when we remember to listen and remind ourselves that each student is unique. Everyone does not learn the same way at the same time — and there are multiple ways to measure content mastery and worthiness for college admission. Todd's research is palpable and worthy.

There are significant individuals whom we hold in high esteem because they remind us that, even though data analytics is seemingly morphing college admission into a business model, we know that it does still remain a people process, too. There are Directors of Admission we particularly trust who keep us alert to pending issues of concern. For instance, when

Bill Fitzsimmons at Harvard speaks to us, we listen. When Rick Clark at Georgia Tech shares his data — from research on testing to Artificial Intelligence, we learn. When Rick Shaw at Stanford clarifies conflicting perceptions, we sigh with relief. When Lee Coffin at Dartmouth relates to us that he is reading in context, we take note. When Ivar Moller at The University of St. Andrews in Scotland connects with us, we confirm compelling issues abroad. When Jon Boeckenstedt at Oregon State goes on his Twitter rants about current educational practices, we question them along with him.

We are discerning consumers of media, as well, and choose the folks we listen to with great care. When Scott Jaschik at *Inside Higher Ed* trumpets his nuanced investigative reports, we pay attention. When Jeff Selingo analyzes shifting trends in admission, we read his tomes and smile at him with renewed appreciation for the individuals who must navigate the projective analytics that have come to confound so many. As to the science that informs us, where would we be without what we continue to learn from Howard Gardner's insight about "how children think and how schools should teach."

From admission directors, to college presidents, to media we trust, to research we garner, we stay close to the issues that keep our teens on edge, working to mitigate their stress and helping them secure their future.

We acknowledge with appreciation the support our family has offered, sustaining without complaint — mostly — the late (sometimes missed!) dinners they have endured due to our focus on our students and our pursuit of the best guidance we can offer to confused parents and anxious teens trying to find their way.

We offer heart-felt thanks to the multitude of folks who have sent us such kind notes of deep appreciation for how we have helped them get through this arduous process of college admission. We have always said our goal is to have family members still love each other at the end of the process!

We write in the hope that you, too, will experience a paradigm shift in how you think about and take charge of your education and the way you shape your experiences.

Remember, we invite you to get past the media hype that can startle and unsettle and confuse. Assemble thinking partners that you trust, those who are grounded in current data. We thank profusely and frequently the multitude of colleagues with whom we have worked, learned, and celebrated over the years! So many decisions and choices are now based on data analytics — a worthy source if you remain a discerning consumer and find your own truth as you sort through the musings and dig into the research, much of which qualifies as empirically grounded, some of which is skewered as a result of partially altered statistics, whether intentionally or otherwise.

Education has always been at the forefront of priorities for our family — and we want the best that the world has to offer for our progeny, whether institutionally-guided or self-directed. Our forebearers and our life experiences have confirmed for us that education is the one thing that stays with us, regardless of economic or philosophical or political upheaval. So often, we see generational shifts in our students where, over time, a family's educational priorities can get muffled, diluted, become hazy — albeit, obscured or even forgotten as a goal to achieve, a priority to clutch and to keep close. Each generation has its challenges and priorities; history attests to that factoid — regardless of which version (or revision) of history one is currently reading. We hold to the value of an individual's being in charge of his or her own destiny.

We seldom succeed alone. Building bridges matters. The world will not come to you. You must reach out and connect. Listen intently and act with utmost urgency and anticipation. Listen and take charge. It's up to you.

This Photo Courtesy of David Shutts Photography

ABOUT THE AUTHORS

Judith Widener Muir – B.A., M.Ed., Ed.M., CEP

Judy has worked with families and independent schools around the world for over thirty years. Managing expectations is a key component in serving students and their families. Muir's early training at the Gesell Institute of Child Development at Yale shaped the lens through which she views education, focusing on the process a child manifests in problem-solving and skill-building. A later degree as an Educational Diagnostician and Reading Specialist added clinical tools to her assessments of student progress.

As head of a Sacred Heart lower school for girls and then a school for children with learning differences, Judy empowered teachers to individualize instruction to meet the wide range of learners in their classrooms. She has designed curriculum for teachers and parents of children demonstrating exceptional potential for the Department of Education in Washington, DC. Judy served for twelve years as the Associate Director of College Counseling at The Kinkaid School in Houston, where she was also the Director of a high-powered internship program for thirty years, placing over 130 seniors each January in three-week internship positions around the globe.

Judy combines a double English and History Major from The College of Wooster with a Master's Degree and Professional Certifications from The University of Houston. Judy also holds a Graduate Degree from Harvard University in Mind, Brain and Education which investigates cognitive development, genetics, neuroscience from infancy through early adulthood and their relationship to learning and education. She was a Teaching Fellow at Harvard's Graduate School of Education for eight years, where she commuted one day each week from Houston to help teach a class in Educational Neuroscience. She sits on the National Editorial Advisory Group for *The Fiske Guide to Colleges* and is a member of NACAC, TACAC, a Professional Member of IECA, and a Certified Educational Planner.

Katrin Muir Lau – B.A., M.A., CEP, Sotheby's Graduate Program: NYC

Katrin, as the daughter of an experienced and highly-recognized college counselor, has been exploring college locations and the application process for decades. Family vacations provided an opportunity to visit yet another college campus along the way, and dinner conversations centered on the nuances of a campus or a college's decision to admit or deny. Katrin's educational and professional journey has kept her focused on seeing beyond the obvious and communicating with poignant details. She has worked at The National Gallery of Art in Washington, DC, and at Sotheby's in both Washington, DC, and New York City. She has also created an interdisciplinary, project-based Art History curriculum and matched families to homes and antiques through Christie's international offerings. She now uses those skills in the arena of college counseling. As an artist, published photographer, art historian, and former varsity athlete, Katrin combines her expertise in college admissions with a personal understanding of how students must craft their story to gain a seat at the college that will provide the best fit.

In her previous positions as College Counselor and Director of College Counseling at independent day schools, Katrin has advised multiple international families, helping students navigate applications to England, Scotland, Canada, Germany, Spain, Norway, Singapore, Japan and Australia — all with very different procedures. International families continue to seek her advice. Katrin also works with top athletic recruits — coordinating the efforts of students, parents, and coaches, guiding them through NCAA eligibility requirements — to achieve their athletic aspirations.

A graduate in Art History from Southern Methodist University, Katrin also holds a Master's Degree in Education from The University of Texas at Austin, and a Graduate Degree in American Decorative Arts from Sotheby's, New York City. Additionally, she holds Certificates for further study of College Admission through the Harvard Summer Institute, The College Board, IECA Summer Training Program, and the University of California. She sits on the National Editorial Advisory Group for *The Fiske Guide to Colleges* and is a member of NACAC, TACAC, a Professional Member of IECA, and a Certified Educational Planner. She and her husband live in Houston, and they have two current college students.

Judy Muir and Katrin Lau are based in Houston, Texas. Families from around the globe seek their direction in managing the complex college admission process that seems to lack transparency. Emerging high schools from around the world also call them to develop their college counseling program — to hire and train staff, to develop the school's profile, to connect them to colleges. Existing high schools seek them out to retool their programs and make them more effective in promoting personal growth.

Wherever you are in the college admissions process, they can help you make the elusive process manageable, keep you steady, and help you emerge with your relationships intact. They can help you present your Authentic U.

www.educationalplan.com

ABOUT THE PHOTOGRAPHER

Robert Ellis Muir

Rob Muir is recognized nationally as one of the leading architectural photographers of our time. He creates images that communicate, win awards, and get published.

Mentored by the great photographer Ansel Adams — spending time with him in Yosemite and Carmel, Rob still remembers the master's words: "You have an eye for light and composition. Go home and start your own business." Muir took Adams' advice.

Rob Muir morphs classical training and cutting-edge technology into images that speak to an audience. Muir's photography has helped his clients win hundreds of local, state, and national awards for their products and services, enhancing their brands and leading to millions of dollars in sales.

Muir is a graduate of the St. John's School, Houston; The College of Wooster, Ohio — with a triple major in History, English, Art; and The Banff School of Fine Arts, Canada. Muir is an avid sailor.

He is married to Judy Muir. They have three children and nine grandchildren.

GLOSSARY

Apprentice - a person who is learning from a career professional.

Apprentice Model - working/studying under a master in a career field.

Apprentice's Secret - putting the fire of learning in your heart; being a lifelong learner to maintain a fulfilling life of purpose.

Co-op, Cooperative Education - intermingling stretches of professional employment or internships, generally a paid experience, within academic coursework.

Delayed Start (to College) - pausing beginning official study on campus by spending the first semester or the first year in pursuit of a worthy experience, either for learning or for service. Can be a personal choice or a provisional offer of admission from a college. Often a marketing strategy, enabling a college to offer more acceptances and to have a vetted wait list for the following year to accommodate potential "freshman melt."

Experiential Learning - learning by doing, beyond memorization and reading, and applying what you already know. A great way to differentiate and to find your best fit as you plan and secure your future.

Externship - a student goes through a partnership with their school and other companies to learn practical experiences but doesn't necessarily do daily tasks within the job. Generally a short-term experience, an introduction to a field that a student is exploring.

Global Scholar - adding an abroad program to an academic regime during college years, combining academic and cultural experiences to enrich learning and expand understanding of the contemporary challenges; plus learning to work across differences, often collaboratively.

Informational Interview - a conversation with a professional that helps you learn about their career.

Intern - a student working with a professional to learn about their organization or their trade, investigating a potential future personal fit.

Internship - spending a length of time along-side a professional to learn about their company and their career, working on daily assignments by completing tasks or projects and attending meetings. An internship can last a few hours to a few months and can be paid or unpaid or sometimes funded by an organization or a college.

Lunch - a meal where you can spend time with a mentor, and hope to stay after to walk around their office with them to learn about their company or their career path.

Maker Studio - a designated place where engineers, in particular, or (hopefully) any range of students in an array of majors, can produce innovative projects.

Mentor - a person who will share their knowledge with another person about what they do and why they love it.

Project - a designated activity that drives learning about a topic or a career path, often with a finished product at the conclusion that manifests learning or solving a designated problem.

Project-Based Learning - using projects to discover new connections, rather than merely reading about them vicariously.

Research - digging into new information, seeking new knowledge, relevant to a topic you are investigating, often scholarly or artistic.

Resume - a document in which you can highlight all of your activities, honors and accolades on for a college or an employer.

Service Learning - applying what you are learning in useful ways within a community through service, combining learning and service simultaneously.

Shadow - meeting a person in their professional office to follow them around for the day.

Tufts University – Medford, Massachusetts

END NOTES

Following are the Readings and Research that have informed and inspired us and grounded the messages in the first half of this book.

Rose, T. The end of average: How we succeed in a world that values sameness. (2016) New York. HarperCollins. pp. 1-191.

Eagleman, D. (2011). Incognito: The secret lives of the brain. New York. Pantheon Books. pp. 1-225.

Mazur, E. (2012).The twilight of the lecture. Harvard Magazine. Retrieved from: http://harvardmagazine/com/2012/03/twilight-of-the-lecture.

Medina, J. (2008). Brain rules. Seattle, WA: Pear Press. pp.29-70.

Learning, whether in a classroom or beyond, is highly personal, driven by intellectual curiosity, initiative, and relevance. Science now confirms that students learn best in meaningful relationships with people who care. Todd Rose, a colleague who is a Harvard professor and widely published author, has inspired us by providing research about how education is due for a make-over, as we have moved from an industrial to a knowledge and now even to a tech-based company economy. Todd purports in his research and publications, such as *The End Of Average*, that everyone does not learn at the same pace in the same way and that we need to individualize instruction to meet learners where they are, paying attention to individual needs, goals, interests, and learning styles. Given the digital landscape where we now reside, these changes can happen readily. This revelation about the power of self-directed learning, initiated by an individual in a personally relevant specialty area, confirms the impact individuals can have on moving their careers forward. Dig into Todd Rose publications to learn more.

As current education comes under fire about how it is not preparing students adequately for the world they will enter, self-directed learning takes on momentum and is supported by scientific discovery. Students must pick up the slack on their own.

The digital landscape provides new sets of educational tools beyond academic circles. Udacity, Khan Academy, Coursera and college webinars from Harvard to MIT to Stanford offer ways to enrich self-directed learning, offering hope and opportunity. Articles in *The Chronicle of Higher Education* and *Inside Higher Ed* also provide current perspectives on pivotal educational issues.

Mentoring remains a meaningful tool to connect and grow in a one-on-one learning environment — a clarion call for an individual yearning to advance skills, academic and personal alike. In addition, new experiences through mentoring expand brain circuitry. David Eagleman introduced us to the concept of neural lightning storms and lightning-fast circuits in our brains. We suggest reading his provocative book *Incognito* to understand better how the brain automates and ties new experiences to past events in the name of efficiency. "Just-in-time learning" (*Incognito*, p. 71) is much of what an intern must do with a mentor to maximize their learning and stay engaged in the process, essentially rewiring brain circuits to accomplish a task with maximum efficiency.

John Medina has a zingy way of relating his research on his website and in his books, such as *Brain Rules*, which provide quotable insight worthy of noting in the section that confirms how experiences shape the architecture of brain development.

Richardson, W. (2010). Blogs, wikis, podcasts, and other powerful web tools for classrooms. Thousand Oaks, CA: Corwin. pp. 1-160.

Richardson, W. and Mancabelli, R. (2011). Personal learning networks: Using the power of connections to transform education. Bloomington, IN: Solution Tree Press. pp. 1-142.

Vygotsky's research is inspirational, as well. His research incorporates scaffolding techniques and problem-solving methods that can result in dynamic decision making, again showing the merit and positive results of self-directed learning, often as a component of and complement to formal education, immediately applicable to moving ahead on a career path.

Vygotsky, L. Zone of proximal development, mind and society: The development of higher psychological processes. (1978). Cambridge, MA: MIT Press.

Vygotsky, L. Thought and Language. (1986). Cambridge, MA: MIT Press. pp. 190-208.

Howard Gardner, Harvard professor and author whose books appear in multiple languages, addresses the many ways intelligence can be recognized and nurtured. His research and message expand our thinking about the many ways we can assess content mastery and define personal aptitudes and potential, reinforcing a reason to move ahead with self-directed learning to identify and measure the fit for a potential career, causing us to rethink how we define success and set goals.

Gardner, H. (2000). Intelligence reframed: Multiple intelligences for the 21st century. New York: Basic Books.

Gardner, H. (2004). Changing minds: The art and science of changing our own and other people's minds. Boston: Harvard Business School Press.

Gardner, H. (2004). The unschooled mind: How children think and how schools should teach, NY: Basic Books.

Gardner, H. (2006). Five minds for the future. Cambridge: Harvard Business School Press.

Gopnik, A. (2012). What's wrong with the teenage mind? Wall Street Journal. January 28, Section C, p. 1.

Hallowell, E. (2006). Crazy Busy: Overstretched, overbooked, and about to snap. NY: Ballentine Books. pp. 1-229.

Kegan, R. & Lahey, L. (2001). How the way we talk can change the way we work. San Francisco, CA: Jossey-Bass. pp. 1-227.

Kegan, R. & Lahey, L. (2009). Immunity to change: How to overcome it and unlock the potential in yourself and your organization. Boston: Harvard Business Press. pp. 1-64.

McEwen, B. & Lasley, E. (2002). The end of stress as we know it. New York: Dana Press. pp. 1-202.

Stress is the hallmark of the college application process where teens feel they have little to no control over outcome.

McEwen, B. (2012). The ever-changing brain; Cellular and molecular mechanisms for the effects of stressful experiences. DEV NEUROBIOLOGY. 72(6). pp. 878-890.

Muir, J. (2012). Live wires: Neuro-parenting to ignite your teen's brain. Houston: Bright Sky Press. pp. 1-160.

Piaget, J. (1952[1936]). The origins of intelligence in children. International University Press.

Sapolsky, R. (2004). Why zebras don't have ulcers: An updated guide to stress, stress related diseases, and coping (3rd ed.). New York: Owl Books.

Reflect on the history of education itself. Collegiate teaching was based on the classics and enrolled those primarily heading towards a position in law, medicine, or the clergy. Scientific learning often came through itinerant lecturers or scientific societies. James Watt, a surveyor and instrument maker, and Nathaniel Bowditch, an astronomer, both largely self-educated. come to mind. Bowditch apprenticed to a merchant who sold supplies to ships and read profusely from calculus to philosophy. He constructed a barometer and wrote a book on marine navigation that still lands on American seafaring vessels today. History is replete with people who reached out with their own self-directed learning. It was up to them to shape it, pursue it, apply it. And they did.

Bowditch, N. The new American practical navigator. (1802). Edmund M. Blunt, original publisher. Rights to book purchased by United States Navy. 60 revised editions. Book now referred to as BOWDITCH.

Mentoring builds relationships that are pivotal. Shawn Achor reveals the power of personal connections, reinforcing the power of mentoring relationships in particular. His focus on positivity is inspirational and anchored in his research. Carol Dweck's growth mindset still permeates educational research at Stanford. Ben-Shahar taught Harvard's famous happiness classes which drew huge numbers of students. These three authors remind us that we are inherently social entities seeking meaningful connections.

Achor, S. Big potential: How transforming the pursuit of success raises our achievement, happiness, and well-being. (2018). New York. Penguin Random House. pp. 1-231.

Achor, S. The happiness advantage: The seven principles of positive psychology that fuel success and performance at work. (2010). New York. Random House. pp. 1-210.

Ariely, D. Predictably irrational: The hidden forces that shape our decisions. (2008). New York. HarperCollins. pp. 1-244.

Ben-Shahar, T. Happier: Learn the secrets to daily joy and lasting fulfillment. (2007). New York. McGraw-Hill. pp. 1-168.

Ben-Shahar, T. The pursuit of perfect: How to stop chasing perfection and start living a richer, happier life. (2009). New York. McGraw-Hill. pp. 1-228.

Brooks, D. The social animal: The hidden sources of love, character, and achievement. (2011). New York. Random House. pp. 1-376.

Christakis, N. and Fowler, J. Connected: The surprising power of our social networks and how they shape our lives. (2009). New York. Little Brown. pp. 1-306.

Christensen, C. How will you measure your life. (2012). New York. HarperCollins. pp. 1-206.

Christensen, C. and Ewing, H. The innovative university: Changing the dna of higher education from the inside out. (2011). San Francisco. Jossey-Bass. pp. 1-401.

Duckworth, A. Grit: The power of passion and perseverance. (2016). New York. Simon & Schuster. pp. 1-284.

Dweck, C. Mindset: The new psychology of success. (2006). New York. Random House. pp. 1-239.

Furda, E. and Steinberg, J. The college conversation: A practical companion for parents to guide their children along the path to higher education. (2020). New York. Penguin Random House. pp. 1-225.

Gladwell, M. Outliers: The story of success. (2008). New York. Little Brown. pp. 1-285.

Gladwell, M. The penguin and the leviathan: How cooperation triumphs over self-interest. (2011). New York. Random House. pp. 1-249.

Grant, A. Think again: The power of knowing what you don't know. (2021). New York. Penguin Random House. pp. 1-257.

Heath, C. and Heath, D. Switch: How to change things when change is hard. (2010). New York. Random House. pp. 1-268.

Pennebaker, J. (2011). The secret life of pronouns: What our words say about us. New York: Bloomsbury Press. pp. 1-229.

Pentland, A. Social physics: How good ideas spread — the lessons from a new science. (2014). New York. Penguin Press. pp. 1-264.

Pink, D. Drive: The surprising truth about what motivates us. (2009). New York. Penguin Group. pp. 1-215.

Seligman, M. with Reivich, K., Jaycox, L. and Gillham, J. (1995). The optimistic child: A proven program to safeguard children against depression and build lifelong resilience. New York: Houghton Mifflin. pp. 1-305.

Shonkoff, J. and Phillips, D. (Eds.). From Neurons to Neighborhoods: The science of early childhood development. (2000). Washington, DC, National Research Council and Institute of Medicine. National Academy Press. pp. 1-413.

Spooner, J. No one ever told us that: Money and life letters to my grandchildren. (2012). New York. Hachette Book Group. pp. 1-231.

Tardy, A. Why mentoring matters: How smart leaders mobilize relentless leadership (2013). Fishhead Publishing, Red Bank, NJ. pp. 1-54.

Untermeyer, C. How important people act: Behaving yourself in public. (2014). Houston. Bright Sky Press. pp. 1-110.

The College of Wooster requires a senior-year thesis. A biography of Howard Lowry, President of the College, himself a Princeton graduate, became the topic of Judy's thesis. His words about "The Apprentice's Secret" resound with me still. He was a scholar, an author, a dynamic speaker, a student of history who held on to the best of the past while projecting how ideas could adapt to the future. His words continue to inspire me, and I share them with my readers here. Many of the references to apprenticeships I attribute to my study of his writings and speeches, which I still hold in awe, which I still find relevant and worthy.

Blackwood, J. Howard Lowry: A life in education (1975). Wooster, OH. College of Wooster Press. pp. 1-317.

The second half of our book gives readers a road map. Students come to us from around the world with bold aspirations, both seeking entry to highly selective colleges or pursuing jobs with top companies or organizations. Many want the Ivies — Harvard, Princeton, Yale, Columbia, Dartmouth, Brown, U Penn, Cornell — or another top tier school — such as MIT, Stanford, UChicago, Duke — or the flagship state schools — UTexas, Texas A&M, UMichigan, UVA, UNC, UCLA, Berkeley — because they perceive they will have an edge in the employment market upon graduation, targeting the big-name financial firms and tech companies, or creating a competitive start-up right out of the gate.

What they often do not know yet is that colleges and employers are making significant shifts in how they will make decisions — how they are reading applications in context more than ever.

Also included in this section — and throughout the text — are excerpts from what student interns have shared with us as they completed their programs with personally-matched mentors. Their appreciation, remarkable awareness, and personal growth astound us and reinforce repeatedly the impact of engaging with mentors who care. Their insights have filled us with awe, and they became an inspiration for this part of the book.

Once again, self-directed learning is pivotal to outcome.

We follow closely the changes, updates and disruptions in the college admission process and the marketplace of employment and help students be as competitive as possible. This section reflects our continuing research through college publications, counselor updates, conferences, reliable news sources, plus webinars and meetings with our colleagues in the college arena and beyond.

Among the scholars that hold our rapt attention about preserving liberal arts college programs are the following. Each addresses the needs of a democracy, which must have discerning voters to flourish and a continuing supply of trained workers to sustain the economic pipeline. Trends reveal exploding costs and expanding online learning opportunities. As the debate heats up and colleges figure out how to shape their programs, students generally need to launch their careers by going beyond the classroom. Derek Bok, former President of Harvard, and William Bowen, former President of Princeton, and Andrew Delbanco, Professor of Humanities at Columbia, are worthy messengers who inform our thinking and that we recommend you consider investigating as you shape your own perspective on these timely topics. Christianson argues that recent economic turbulence is demanding changes in higher education, a message ringing loud and clear among families frustrated with escalating costs and looking for value in a college education to justify the cost.

Bok, D. (2013). Higher education in America. Princeton: Princeton University Press. pp. 1-412.

Bowen, W. (2013). Higher education in the digital age. Princeton: Princeton University Press. pp. 1-161.

Delbanco, A. (2012). College: What it was, is, and should be. Princeton: Princeton University Press. pp. 1-177.

Christianson, C., Horn, M. & Johnson, C. (2008). Disrupting class: How disruptive innovation will change the way the world learns. New York: McGraw Hill. pp. 1-230.

Christianson, C. & Eyring, H. (2011). The innovative university: Changing the DNA of higher education. San Francisco, CA: Jossey-Bass. p. 7.

Zhao, Yong. (2009). Catching up or leading the way: American education in the age of globalization. Alexandria, VA: ASCD. pp. 1-230.

Zhan, Yong. (2012). World class leaders: Educating creative and entrepreneurial students. Thousand Oaks, CA: Corwin. pp. 1-256.

Science confirms that students learn best in meaningful relationships.

National Scientific Council on the Developing Child. (2oo4). Working Paper No. 1.

The College of Wooster has a particularly well-organized Career Planning Center. They offer materials for students regarding careers and how to pursue them. Replete with lists of potential careers based on majors, information on crafting effective resumes, and how to prepare for interviews, the staff has been bountiful in their time commitment to connecting students with internships, meaningful research, and potential employers. We have found their information informative, well organized and useful. Their materials provided fodder for the chapter on how to use your major. We thank them, and we applaud them for what they are doing to guide and help their students connect with and shape their future! Their work and their presentations are exceptional.

Apex: Advising, Planning, Experiential Learning. Career Planning. The College of Wooster. Gault Library. 1140 Beall Avenue. Wooster, OH 44691. www.wooster.edu/academics/apex

We must also recognize High Point University (HP), which trumpets the way that students can "earn success and discover significance" through the training they receive there. President Nido R. Qubein teaches a remarkable Freshman Seminar on Life Skills. High Point listens to the marketplace and has brought in programs, facilities, and staff that have combined to grow enrollment exponentially. Deemed a Life Skills University, HP shows a 97% employment/continuing education rate following graduation. How do they achieve these stats? Teaching course content that is relevant and amassing real world experiences. HP offers many directives: internships, practical advice from successful mentors, research, connections with global leaders, and learning to work across differences to achieve common goals. HP "embraces the world as it is and as it is going to be with a growth mindset that penetrates the minds, hearts and souls of their students." HP offers "a brilliant blend of academic innovation, real work practicality, and personal values." The university and its students are flourishing! Their model is inspiring. We thank them and celebrate what they are achieving. In fact, on our last visit to their campus, we arrived as a deluge of rain was just passing through and looked up to see a sweeping rainbow stretching across their campus. We smiled — and thought, how appropriate!

High Point University: A Life Skills University. One University Parkway. High Point, N.C. highpoint.edu

We recommend the following sources that have been useful to us and that are reflected in this section, as well.

Selingo, J. Who gets in and why: A year inside college admissions. (2020). Simon & Schuster. pp. 1-267.

Selingo, J. College (un)bound: The future of higher education and what it means for students. (2013). New York. Houghton Mifflin Harcourt. pp. 1-212.

Selingo, J. There is life after college: What parents and students should know about navigating school to prepare for the jobs of tomorrow. (2016). New York. HarperCollins. pp. 1-263.

Lau, K. and Muir, J. Finding your u: Navigating the college admission process. (2015). Houston: Bright Sky Press. pp. 1-126.

Muir, J. Live wires: Neuro-parenting to ignite your teen's brain. (2012). Houston, Bright Sky Press. pp. 1-130.

Lieber, R. The price you pay for college: An entirely new road map for the biggest financial decision your family will ever make. (2021). New York. HarperCollins. pp. 1-316.

Horn, M. and Staker, H. Blended: Using disruptive innovation to improve schools. (2015). San Francisco. Jossey-Bass. pp. 1-293.

Pope, D. and Brown, M. and Miles, S. Overloaded and underprepared: Strategies for stronger schools and healthy, successful kids. (2015). San Francisco. Jossey-Bass. pp. 1-218.

Wagner, T. Creating innovators: The making of young people who will change the world. (2012). New York. Simon & Schuster. pp. 1-251.

INDEX

INDEX

INDEX

NOTES

NOTES

NOTES

Columbia University – New York City